MYSTIC MOMMY

Cat RunningElk

Mystic Mommy
Knowing Who You Are, Why You're Here and What
You're Going to Do About It

ISBN: 0-9767094-0-6

Library of Congress Cataloging-in-Publication Data
RunningElk,Cat
Mystic Mommy: knowing who you are, why you're here
and what you're going to do about it
2005903119

Published by
RunningElk Publishing
Sedona, Arizona

First Printing, 2005

Cover Design: Kathi Dunn, www.duhn-design.com
Mountain Lion Illustration: Christopher Jackson

This book is dedicated to
Lauren, Grace and Amber.
My patience, my hope and my joy.

ACKNOWLEDGEMENTS

Since the beginning, there have been teachers. We all have them, but sometimes do not recognize them. I would like to recognize a few very important teachers in my life.

To Stephanie Kacena, you helped me open the window. This story really begins with our meeting. Thank you for your wisdom and healing touch. To Marilyn Wolffe, you said in one year I would be doing the things you do. Well, it's taken me much longer than that! Thank you for recognizing me the first day we met. To Dee and Valerie, thank you for your guidance. To Kyle Anne McIntyre, the student was ready and you were there. Thank you for all you taught me. Thank you for showing me how to be true to who I am.

Thanks to the Dolphin House, in Kingston, Washington. To everyone at those first psychic fairs and to Vita, for showing up. Bless you all. Love to the teachers who led me to Gangaji; Christopher Love, Michael Felker and special thanks to Peggy Jordan. Thanks for pushing me over the edge. If not for you I might have stood looking at that cliff a long time.

To Ted, thank you for ushering me to the threshold. You taught me to lighten up and have always been able to get me to laugh. And that's a very serious thing!

My first teachers, this time around, have been my mother, Arlene, my sister, Tamra, my Aunt Rogene, and my grandmothers, who have passed over. You taught me unconditional love as well as how to be strong, resilient and forgiving. Thank you. To the women of CALM BULC, Megan Turner, Susan Fossen and Robyn Lawrence, you are so special to me. To everyone at ARTS in Kansas City. You have all been such a support and inspiration to me. Megan Cramer, thank you. A great writer, editor and ear. William Guilkey, thank you for your loving help. Karen Watson, thank you for your courage and honesty. Thanks to Duke Tufty, Karyn Bradley and everyone at Unity Temple. Graham and Susan at Write to Your Market, you are amazing. Kathi and Hobie at Dunn and Associates, thank you for your inspiring work. Lee Glickstein, your work has allowed me to use my voice, again. Thank you. G. W. Hardin, thank you for listening. Lynn V. Andrews, thank you for your words.

To Christopher Jackson, thank you for your love, first and foremost. Thank you for your hard work on this project. Thank you for the priceless photos and for the incredible experience at Turpentine Creek - touching a real mountain lion. Dreams really do come true. You have touched the mountain lion, and forever changed her.

And the three greatest teachers to come into my life are my daughters. You three are my inspiration and joy and together you embody all the wisdom of the world. You were the reason I began the search. With all my heart and soul, this one's for you.

MYSTIC MOMMY

I feel myself drift off into a trancelike state...

In the body of a healthy, full-grown male elk, I run up the mountain before me. With strength and assuredness I climb. I hear the snorting sounds of others behind me. My attention turns to the one behind me and now I find myself in the body of another elk, female this time. She is close behind the stag before her. My feet carefully land on rocks as I duck beneath tree branches. We dart here and there, following the quickest path to...

I hear more breathing behind me and as my attention shifts so does my form, into the body of yet another elk cow. She is following the two in front of her. There is a sense of urgency and as the pace quickens I hear a hissing breath behind me and the spine tingling cry of...

I am the hunter — mountain lion. The hooves of the elk are only a heartbeat away. With fire in my veins I follow my passion...

CHAPTER ONE

MYSTIC MESSAGES

S ince I was very young I've paid close attention to my dreams because I knew they were a gift. If I could understand their meanings, I could foretell my future. Sometimes they have told me more than I wanted to know, for they have always reflected to me what might be.

But this time that woman was speaking to me in a language I couldn't understand. What was she trying to tell me?

In this dream I saw mothers and children walking along a wide path. All of them were going in the same direction.

There were mothers of all nationalities and it seemed as though every race was represented.

Every woman had a child, or two, or many. The smaller children hung onto skirts or were riding in carriers against their mothers' backs or breast. Some women walked and talked with others. Some kept to themselves while looking ahead.

I saw pilgrim women, Victorian ladies and gypsies wearing colorful skirts and jewelry that jingled. There were tribal women with the simplest coverings over their almost naked bodies, their skin dark and glowing with oils. They kept their babies wrapped tightly against them, skin to skin. I saw women dressed modestly in puritan clothing, their children running and playing in stuffy wool trousers or dresses with layers of petticoats beneath. The children ranged in age from the tiniest babe suckling a breast to boys and girls well into puberty.

All of the women were Mothers. Mothers with their children. Children ran, walked, skipped, had fun, somberly followed, led, or just hung on. I watched them as they came streaming by me. It was like watching through a hidden camera. They didn't notice me, neither the mothers, nor their children.

MYSTIC MOMMY

Then this woman stepped off the path and came toward me. She was black-skinned and wore a sarong of brilliant reds and golds. On both her arms were cuff-like bracelets, and her neck was wrapped heavily in beaded necklaces, one after another extending halfway down her chest. She carried a baby on one hip and a slightly older child hung onto her skirt. She turned toward me, as if I was the camera-woman. She came in closer and closer to my lens. Her green emerald eyes stood out in sharp contrast to her dark-as-night skin. Her penetrating stare drew me in.

She wasn't smiling, but a deep sincerity radiated from her as she stared long and hard. She understood something about me, or something I was going through.

Who are you? I said within my own head...*What do you want?*

She spoke to me as if she could hear my thoughts. There was a passionate fire in her voice, yet her demeanor remained balanced, even with the baby on one hip.

"Wa nonee moh jah wo eh Lay oh."

Her words were foreign but I felt something beyond the language. I thought perhaps she was telling me about the children - hers - or maybe mine.

"Ma ko wawa kay shoh be nobe in zhen."

What are you trying to tell me? I really want to understand...

"Kay shoh mbee lee eh tah too mah mah..."

Her strong tone and penetrating eyes sent me spinning and instantly I find myself back in my body lying on my bed. Her stare was like a camera flash that kept repeating, even as I opened my eyes and looked around my bedroom her eyes seemed to still be there, watching me.

Chills ran up and down my spine.

What was she trying to tell me? I felt a deep urgency within her words. And the intensity of her eyes I'd never forget.

I knew there was special significance in all those mothers and my own path of motherhood. All those mothers were just following one another in a steady stream.

I'm a mother, too. A mother with a daughter less than two years old and a second daughter my husband and I are adopting from India. Like my mother and my mother's mother, and on and on before them - I am giving my life to my family - to my child and soon to both of my daughters. It's how it's always been.

My mother sacrificed her own dreams for her family. She was there for us - she gave. She was a mother.

And now I am a part of that stream. I am a part of the stream of women with children to raise. Am I just blindly following along the path of my mother? Will it be any different for me than it was for her? Is this what God, Spirit, the Universe, wants me to do? Or is there something more? Is there something more Spirit wishes me to know? Is there something more for me to do?

This woman stepped out of the line to speak to me. Perhaps she was *THE Earth Mother* come to bless me. Anxiously I am awaiting the arrival of my second child. She will be arriving from India soon, I hope. Perhaps this woman was blessing me and my new daughter...

I tucked the memory away, not wanting to consider the truth I heard in the woman's tone. It wasn't a blessing - it was a warning. I didn't want to think about it. My daughter was coming from India.

CHAPTER TWO

WAITING FOR GRACE

Dreamtime: *I am sitting in a circle of women, some of them I know - an aunt and my grandmother - and many more I do not recognize. A feeling of love and protection emanates from each of these wise women toward me and my baby.*

In my waking reality I am pregnant with my second child. Inside of me a baby is growing, but in the dream a fetus is clinging to the outside of my body. The fetus is totally exposed with no womb to protect it. It shimmies up my chest and nestles its tiny, wet head under my chin. Then the tiny baby lies contentedly, waiting.

A large hand reaches down and begins to pull the child away from me. The baby clutches my skin and clings tightly to me. It begins to cry.

Sensing the baby's fright as well as my own   I cry out, "NO!"

The hand speaks to me in a powerful voice, neither feminine nor masculine: "This isn't the way."

Then again this hand from above is pulling on my child, trying to wrestle it free from my body..

My baby is crying wildly now and I scream even louder this time, "NO! Don't take my baby!"

The hand removes the tightly clinging baby and says again, "This isn't the way."

I am scared and concerned about what is happening to my baby. Then I hear, "You'll get her back."

I awake in the morning shaking, and I know I have lost the baby inside of me. By noon I am bleeding.

Of course I am devastated by my loss, but I cling to the words from my dream, the voice said: "You'll get her back."

MYSTIC MOMMY

At first I didn't know how, or when. I focused on my own healing and I trusted the way would be revealed to me. A few months later I saw an ad in the paper for an informational meeting on adoption. My husband and I didn't even have to discuss it. We had talked about the possibility of adopting someday, and we knew in our hearts this was the time.

Shortly after that meeting on adoption my husband was watching a television show that talked about a desperate situation in India with baby girls. They aren't wanted, aren't valued as highly as boys. Many women in poor families find it necessary to kill their babies or put them in cribs set outside hospitals and orphanages. The first daughter gets the dowry, if there is money for one, and that is the only way to have them married. If there is no dowry, they cannot be married, they cannot work and many end up as prostitutes or slaves. Not having anywhere to turn, mothers give up their own babies.

I was bathing Lauren when Ted walked into the bathroom. His face was pale from the atrocities he had just seen. I looked in his eyes and saw tears.

Quietly he told me about the television show and then he said: "Let's adopt a girl from India."

I agreed and soon after I listened to our counselor, Shivani, from our adoption agency, tell us why the Indian people did not want my husband and me to adopt a girl. We knew our daughter had to be from India, and we knew it had to be a girl. Besides, the voice had said, "You'll get **her** back."

Shivani told me, "I really don't think we are going to be able to find you a little girl. India would rather place a boy in a home that already has a girl. They feel a second girl will not be loved and cared for and so if you already have a girl they would rather that you adopt a boy. Girls just are not valued as highly in India and they do not understand why you want another girl."

As Shivani finished her dissertation on Indian culture she mentioned, "Well, I do have a file on my desk about a little girl, but she has special needs, and I feel her health is not good, and..."

"Tell me about her," I said feeling my heart quicken.

"She was born at twenty-seven weeks gestation and only two and one half pounds. But it says she was able to maintain her own temperature after only a few days. The nurses did not expect a live birth after the two-day labor. When she was delivered the nurses named her Kripa, which means Grace of God in Hindi. She has Hepatitis B and is anemic."

"What do we do if we are interested in adopting her?"

"I'll send you the file. Please look it over carefully. Do not make a hasty decision. Have a doctor look at her medical records and then let me know. Meantime, I will let you know if anything else opens up."

Days later I tore open the envelope and looked at the picture of tiny Kripa, eyes closed, thin arm raised over her head. Her face looked pale in comparison to the lovely wheat color of her arms.

Her eyes were deep and dark; her entire being was thin and frail looking. To anyone else she might have looked like a very sick child, but to me she was the most beautiful angel I had seen since the birth of my daughter, Lauren.

I began to cry, then I noticed the date of her birth: April 15, 1994. Lauren was born on April 16, 1992. That was all I needed to know. Kripa was my daughter.

Not only was her birthday the day before Lauren's, but after studying my journals, I realized that her conception was the same time or shortly after my miscarriage. I remember the dream telling me "This isn't the way," and "You'll get her back." I know this is my daughter.

We told Shivani to begin the paperwork to bring Kripa, or Grace, as we would call her, home.

As I prepared for the arrival of my second child, I thought this was what my life was meant to be - totally devoted to my family as wife and mother. But my life was about to take an entirely different path. In time the mystical moments I had encountered now and then would grow into a steadier stream of uncanny coincidences. These mystical moments would forever change me. My true callings were beginning.

When Shivani called to tell us the red tape was finally cleared and that Kripa was definitely on her way home I began announcing to everyone, "My baby is coming! My baby is coming!" This affirmation resulted in my body responding as if I were really giving birth. I became ill, nauseated and was cramping twenty-four hours prior to Kripa's arrival. Weak and exhausted but high on adrenaline I stood outside customs, waiting for her arrival. My husband, Ted, my daughter, Lauren, my mother and stepfather and I had all made the trip to the Minneapolis International Airport from Cedar Rapids, Iowa to meet our daughter. An escort was bringing her from Delhi.

Mystic Mommy

As we stood waiting we watched many other travelers come through the double doors. The customs area was completely concealed from our view so we waited not knowing how soon she would be coming.

Soon two flight attendants came through the doors, they looked up and down the long line of people waiting for loved ones. "Where's the mother?" one of the flight attendants called out loudly.

I knew they were looking for me and I raised my hand. From the doorway they began talking to me and continued as they walked down the runway. All the others waiting there in line heard about our daughter.

"Your daughter is so adorable!" one of them cooed.

"What a good baby! She smiled the whole time!" the other flight attendant jumped in excitedly.

"I fell in love with her and I don't even like children!" remarked the first with a laugh.

A small crowd gathered and asked us questions. Soon everyone around us knew we were waiting for our daughter and that we would be meeting her for the first time.

My eyes filled with tears as the flight attendants shared with me details of the last leg of the trip, from Norway to Minneapolis. Then they remained standing nearby so they could see us receive our daughter.

I stood waiting, thinking of my baby, when I felt a sensation in my breasts I hadn't felt since Lauren was a tiny baby. I was lactating. I quickly crossed my arms over my chest to conceal any leakage and hurried to the restroom to check. Yes, it was real, my milk was there. My body believed, or knew, my baby was near.

The escort and our daughter were the last to clear customs. By then a large crowd had gathered. Word of our new daughter had traveled in the terminal and to all the passengers who had been on the plane with Kripa, and so it seemed everyone was hanging around to see the homecoming.

Perry, the escort, came through the double doors carrying Kripa high in the air for everyone to see. Wide eyed tiny Kripa looked out on her audience. Perry seemed to know where to go for magically he walked up to me and handed her across the velvet ropes.

Clapping, cheering and sniffling surrounded me as I took her into my arms. My family and I gathered close together and took turns holding our new child. Just ten months old but so tiny and fragile looking. She had been through so much already, yet I knew she was a strong soul, a strong child.

The nurses in India had named her Kripa, which means "Grace of God," so we called her 'Grace.' Amazing how God, Spirit, the Universe - whatever name you want to call It - had brought her back. The voice had said, "You'll get her back." And I had.

CHAPTER THREE

CR2✵TS✵GY2↻

WHO'S THAT IN THE MIRROR?

G race came home and Lauren adored her little sister.
It was an easy transition for her.

I found myself giving one hundred and fifty percent of
myself to my daughters and never considered my own
needs. Grace's schedule was erratic for awhile with all
the changes she had been through. She was awake most
of the night and I rocked her and sang to her. During the
day I took care of Lauren and Grace, cooked and cleaned.
And of course there was a lot of time spent enjoying my
daughters - laughing, playing, singing and dancing was
also daily fare. The usual mothering stuff.

A few weeks after Grace came home I found myself not feeling very well, but as with any new baby in the house I considered it normal. The fact that I often felt dizzy and had a scratchy throat didn't concern me. Nor did I become concerned when I started dropping glasses, watching them shatter on the kitchen floor because I had misjudged the edge of the counter. None of my own maladies concerned me, but when Grace's nose began to run, I ran to the doctor.

"It's just a cold, nothing to worry about," our family doctor said to me, putting my mind at ease.

"Now let me take a look at you, Juli." He began checking my eyes, ears and throat. I was so tired I didn't protest or ask questions.

I was mildly curious when he checked my balance and we both noticed how difficult it was for me to maintain any. He then took a throat culture and quickly came back to tell me the news.

"Juli, have you been taking care of yourself? Or just these two healthy girls?"

"Well...I..."

"Yes, well. You're about seventy-five percent

dehydrated, you have an inner ear infection and are walking around with bronchitis. I think perhaps you need to take better care of yourself. "

I stared at him as if he were crazy. Didn't he know I was a mother? "I have a new baby! And Lauren just two and Grace isn't sleeping at night and..."

"Take care of yourself – for them!"

Feeling ashamed I silently took the prescription he handed me and headed home with my two healthy children.

How do other women do it? It seems so impossible sometimes. I need to take care of them, and sometimes I just **forget** *about me.*

I knew I needed to make some changes, but what, and how? How could I take care of myself and make sure all their needs were met?

Then I considered the statement Lauren made a few days prior, "I don't like that girl in the mirror," she said pointing to her reflection. She told me she didn't love herself, and it was showing. This was the gift I most wanted to give my daughters. I wanted them to have the self-confidence that had always eluded me, but I was failing. I didn't have it and

I couldn't give it to them.

I showered them both with love, told them how much they were loved and how special they were, over and over again. But maybe that wasn't enough. What if they followed in my footsteps, always looking for love and approval outside themselves? What if they put everyone else first, and never allowed themselves the love and care they deserved?

An angel was waiting for that moment, that moment I finally saw the truth. I needed to heal me first. I couldn't give my daughters something that I didn't have.

I prayed that if I learned to love myself they would learn to do the same.

Putting myself first was a drastic departure from what I thought was good mothering. How selfish! How terrible! What would everyone think?

My husband supported me in taking what looked like small steps for womankind. He knew they were large steps for me. I hoped a few times out of the house to do something for me would be enough. I never imagined it would turn into a mystical calling. There was a need to stop and discover who *I am* – but I didn't know that. I didn't know I was going to discover far more than that, I was also going to discover who I was before.

My first small step was a massage. I scheduled it for June 28, my birthday - my thirtieth birthday. Guilt weighed me down as I prepared to leave my totally capable husband and daughters at home to go have the massage. Standing on the threshold of our front door I nearly broke into tears. Why was it so hard to go out for just a couple of hours? It seemed as though I had lost all of my independence since becoming a stay-at-home mom.

It had only been a few years prior when I was independently living on my own. I had been such a free-spirit. Now I felt insecure about leaving home without my family.

My husband had such a busy schedule – practicing law while attending graduate school. He was studying for his Masters in Education as well as teaching credentials. Unhappy as an attorney, he decided to follow his heart into teaching. He had a lot to do and I was feeling guilty taking time for myself, but it was my birthday.

Ted hugged me and kissed me and then he picked up Lauren. (Grace was sleeping in the playpen behind him.) In his most influentially, cutesy voice he said, "Tell

Mommy to have a relaxing massage. We'll be fine!"

I looked into his eyes, not for reassurance, but out of sheer fright. There was someone deep inside me crying for help and I wanted him to rescue her. I was still looking outside for someone else to help me.

Lauren began to cry as she reached out for me.

I hugged Lauren and started to take her into my arms. She was clinging to me. Or was I clinging to her? Ted pulled her back. "You'll be a better mother. Now GO!"

I felt like it was my first day of kindergarten.

On the way to the massage I turned up the volume on the kind of music I used to listen to before Barney, Big Bird and Winnie the Pooh. As the good-byes faded I felt slightly liberated. Within minutes my nervousness melted away and I began to wonder why I hadn't done this sooner.

Having my first massage was so blissful. Stacie, the woman I had scheduled my appointment with from an ad in the phone book, was a strong, strawberry blond with short hair and wavy curls. She went right to work caressing every inch of my body with love and respect. Self-confidence radiated from her being as she moved knowingly through her routine.

She worked with a gentle strength that relaxed me immediately. I was delighted with the way she magically kept the crisp clean sheet wrapped around my body, exposing only one limb at a time as she carefully and quickly re-wrapped the remaining parts.

The room was lit with candles and the blinds closed out the morning sun. On her CD player was gentle, Native American flute music. Stacie spoke very little and in this relaxing environment, I was able to let go.

At first I only noticed how my body was reacting to her touch. Some parts relaxed immediately as she held my arm or stroked my back. Other areas had surprising pain hidden within them.

Stacie knew where to find these tender spots — along the lines from my shoulders to my ears, down my spine and under my shoulder blades. She knew all the usual places for holding tension. She then touched the inside of my right knee and I cringed at the surprising pain.

"Have you had an injury here?" She said as she kept her hands rotating and ringing around my knee.

"Aaaaah — no — I don't think so...aaah." I tried using the breathing exercises I learned in Lamaze class prior to Lauren's birth to get me through the pain I felt. As she pushed deeper in I suddenly remembered a skiing accident I'd had years before.

The memory came rushing back. Once again I am skiing with friends – all advanced skiers. I'm trying to keep up. I'm losing control as I spot the patch of ice. "NO!" my friends scream! "Don't sit down!" But my instincts wanted to grab onto a piece of earth. Somehow I had to stop!

I'm tumbling, twisting and headed for a ravine, a ravine with trees! I'm coming up from a head over heels tumble and see the tree I am about to hit - SLAM! My eyes popped open as I relived that moment.

"Oh, I forgot all about this. About ten years ago I hit a tree skiing. I hit the inside of that leg and I also nailed the tree here." I rubbed the underside of my jaw. "I was coming out of a head-over-heels spin and luckily was flipping up as I hit the tree or else I..."

"I see." Stacie worked my right knee much longer than she had the left. It hurt but I remained silent, trusting what she was doing was for the best.

MYSTIC MOMMY

Amazingly I'd forgotten all about that accident, but one touch on my knee and zingo! I didn't know it still hurt. While she worked my knee and all the tender space behind it the memories were released. They worked their way from my knee to my mind as I lay there. The skiing accident happened at a major turning point in my life. Or did the accident create an opening for a turning point?

When the ski patrol arrived and looked down into the ravine where I had landed they were surprised I was alive, they later told me. One of the patrol told me that as he looked down at my body lying there he truly believed I was dead. Then my eyes popped open and he said he gasped in shock.

The accident changed my perspective on life. I slowed down. I was young and enjoying life, but the accident shook me up enough to get me to slow down. I partied less and stayed on the easier ski runs. I took in the views more and worried less about keeping up with others.

I also opened up to new ideas about life. A co-worker shared cassette and video tapes with me of a woman who channeled an entity named Ramtha. The idea of channeling was new to me and I was very curious. This 10,000-year-old being used the body and voice of this woman, J.Z. Knight, to communicate with anyone who cared to listen.

Streams of wisdom came through J.Z. and her audiences grew. She had been a housewife, just a housewife. Suddenly one day she found herself able to communicate with an entity named Ramtha. As a result her world was turned upside-down.

The video was fascinating. I began listening to the cassettes everyday. One night after turning off the cassette I felt something very eerie happening. I could feel a presence in my room and it wasn't my roommates, no one else was home. I started to get chills up and down my body. I knew it had to do with the Ramtha tapes and I became very afraid a similar fate might come to me that had happened to J.Z. Knight.

Other beings joined the first. They had messages for me to share. They were speaking directly to me!

Fear ran through my body and I blocked the messages they were sending. I KNEW what they wanted but I didn't allow myself to process it into my conscious thoughts. The beings persisted and I became so overwhelmed I let out a loud, "NO!!!"

The spirits drew back a bit and lifted themselves above me. I knew they were hovering at my ceiling.

"I'M NOT READY!"

I sat down on the bed and cried. Since a young girl I had felt the presence of spirits around me. Like many sensitives, as I became a young adult I found numerous ways to shut out the frightening psychic impressions I felt. Numbing agents like alcohol gave me a false sense of confidence and I felt safe in the darkness they created.

I was trying to keep myself in the dark. I'd been living in darkness for some time and this experience re-awakened a knowing within me. It frightened me. I was living in fear of remembering something ancient within me.

I knew that whatever they wanted to say to me was important. I knew they'd been waiting all my life and I knew listening to Ramtha had caused an opening in my subconscious. Perhaps the accident had shaken me up enough to create a gap...it certainly sobered me up quickly. I wasn't sure how, but I knew there was now a huge opening in the veil and it frightened me.

I wasn't ready. I didn't want to be like J.Z. Knight. I wanted to maintain control over my life and my body. Control? Who was the one skiing off the side of a mountain, completely OUT of control?

Quietly now I bowed my head and folded my hands the way I'd been taught to pray. "Please, just give me a little more time." And suddenly the presence was gone. I felt more alone than ever.

One more time Stacie wrapped her hands around my knee and rung it out like a wet washcloth. The pain was gone completely. So were the frightening memories.

"Boy, she's good." I thought.

The background music changed and a Native American chant began. The chorus of voices called out in their native language. A deep male voice sang in rhythm with the pounding drums. Something buried inside me wanted to sing along.

My eyelids began to flutter and my eyes grew teary. Behind my closed eyelids I saw Stacie working on me as she did here, but she looked quite different. She was in a traditional native deerskin dress with fringe on the sleeves and she knelt next to me as I lay on the ground. I looked into her dark eyes and she smiled warmly back at me. Her hair was black and long. It was the same person, I could tell because with my eyes closed I could feel the same energy healing me here. The same warmth, love, and tenderness pulsated in her strong hands.

How strange, I thought. I wonder where these visions are coming from? Am I imagining this?

More images came quickly. An eagle appeared before me as if to answer my questions. My eyelids fluttered like hummingbird's wings as my eyes followed the eagle into the blue heavens.

As Stacie worked on and around my face and head the eagle flew before me. Then suddenly I was seeing as he did, through his eyes.

I saw a valley and a river far below. I flew to a mountaintop and perched on a rock wall. A gentleman in a white hooded cloak with long gray braids and brown skin greeted me on top of the mountain. He stood to my right and I felt another presence on my left. I was too taken by the elder in white to turn to my left to see what or who stood there. Or perhaps I was afraid to look any farther. As I was looking upon him I changed back into Juli. As I stood in my own body I realized this man, or guide, was at least two or maybe three feet taller than I.

"Longfellow" rang out from his essence and echoed across the canyon below.

"Take a couple minutes to yourself." Stacie tenderly

squeezed the hair on the top of my head and my mind came tumbling back into the room.

She gently shut the door behind her and as the doorknob clicked, my eyes popped open.

Candles flickered in the corners and the drumming played softly from a shelf. Dressing quickly and quietly I noticed the clock on the wall. Two hours had flown by. Had I been here the whole time? It didn't seem possible.

On the wall next to the mirror a certificate stared at me and called me closer. "This certifies that...is a Reiki I Practitioner..." What in the world is 'Reiki?' I wondered.

I moved away from the certificate and looked in the mirror. The reflection I saw was of a totally different woman. The change I felt inside was already apparent to me. I was almost too embarrassed to leave the room, for fear others would notice the peaceful countenance that had overtaken me. "You look like you just had an incredible sexual encounter!" I said to my reflection.

My cheeks were flushed and my eyes twinkled with mystery. I rubbed smeared mascara from under my eyes. My lips remained upturned no matter how hard I tried to keep them neutral. I felt silly and sultry. It wasn't a normal look for me. I didn't usually look so happy and at peace! I tried to comb my hair down with my fingers; my unkempt hair added to the look of an afternoon affair.

I cautiously went to the lobby to speak with Stacie. She sat openly smiling at me as I shared with her some of my experiences during the massage. I was surprised by how much I was willing to share with this total stranger. Strange as it was, she didn't feel like a stranger.

After the massage I was overwhelmed by heightened sensitivities. I heard voices everywhere I went. The checkout clerk at the grocery store wasn't moving her lips but I heard what she was thinking! The same thing happened with the boy putting my grocery bags in the trunk. All he said was "Thank you," but I heard all his plans for after work.

Social events became impossible. There was too much noise! Some people seemed to have more than one voice going on in their heads. I couldn't tell anyone or they immediately became afraid of what I was picking up.

But worst of all were the voices I heard when no one else was around.

***

CHAPTER FOUR

REAWAKENING THE VOICES WITHIN

I continued my massage sessions with Stacie, but after just three or four sessions I found I was receiving more intuitive information than I wanted. I shared with Stacie how I was hearing other people's thoughts and how it was random and certainly not wanted.

"Are you an ultra-sensitive?" she asked.

"Well, I don't know what an ultra-sensitive is, but I am sensitive. My mother has always said I'm *too* sensitive!"

"Do images stay with you from television and movies?"

"Oh! Yes! The news sends me into a depression every night! And scenes from movies play over and over in my mind. I want to erase the scenes but it's so hard."

"You might think about giving up the news. You're an ultra-sensitive all right and watching anything dark, or negative is too much for you. You absorb things easily. You aren't too sensitive, but you are very sensitive, and that's a gift. It will help others once you get a handle on it. For now I'll cut back on the energy work, you don't need so much. And be careful what kind of information you take in." Stacie looked peaceful and calm and there was a twinkle in her eyes as if she understood me oh so well.

She reached in a drawer at the front counter and pulled out some paper.

"I'm giving you the address of a metaphysical shop near here. I think you might find some interesting things there and the women who run it are very friendly. They'll have books for you to read that will help you understand what's going on."

She handed me the paper with the name and address of the store written on it. After saying good-bye I drove straight there. I was anxious to find out more.

MYSTIC MOMMY

I pulled up in front of the old victorian building and contemplated the name of the store. As the friendly women behind the counter asked if they could help...I asked, "So what does Bruja's mean?"

The dark-haired shorter woman looked at the fair-haired taller one, then turned to me and said sweetly, "It means 'wise women.'"

And they certainly turned out to be very wise women. They guided me to books that fit exactly what I was going through.

I whizzed through books on healing and on how our thoughts create our reality; including diseases in the body. I read up on spirit guides, angels and totems. I was soaking it all up and doing it at the same time. I was reading the first chapter of *How to Talk to Your Spirit Guides* by Ted Andrews, when I felt and saw my guides sitting round my bed watching and giggling as I followed the step by step instructions. I tried to ignore them. I wasn't sure if they were real.

I appeared two to three times a week at Bruja's. Sonia and Leah saw me coming and pointed me to the next book, "This one next," they would say handing me a book off the shelf. I would run home and absorb it.

One day I saw a flyer on the bulletin board at Bruja's and I took it down and walked over to ask Sonia and Leah about the spiritual counselor advertised on the flyer.

They nodded knowingly. "Maggie is wonderful. You'll like her."

I felt Maggie would be able to help me with the emotional issues that were still arising from within me. It felt like I was purging old baggage. I had no idea how old that baggage really was.

And maybe, I hoped, she could help me with the voices and spirits that I kept imagining I was seeing and hearing...

"Go see Maggie." One of these spirit guides told me as I drove home from Bruja's.

"I think I'm going crazy." I said to no one, still trying to ignore the spirit guide in the passenger's seat.

Maggie's address was not far from where I lived. I decided to walk to the appointment and enjoyed the beautiful summer day on the way.

My awareness of the world around me seemed greater than usual. Everything was in sharp focus and I noticed every little thing around me.

I spoke with the trees as I walked and felt them communing with me. Stopping to watch squirrels play, I felt giddy and childlike.

As I turned the corner to 19th Street, a busy street no matter the day or the hour, there wasn't a single car in sight. I was surprised there wasn't any traffic in any direction. Everything felt very still and the only movement was my body moving rhythmically down the sidewalk toward my appointment.

"Perhaps I missed something. Everyone has left the planet but I was out of body and missed the whole thing..."

It felt like the universe was watching the one actor on stage: me. The earth had come to a complete stop. Traffic had ceased. I walked for several blocks and still nothing but my own feet moved.

The trees were still, the breeze stopped. The unusual stillness in the air gave me a chill. I looked for squirrels, a dog in a yard, children playing...nothing. Not a soul to be seen up and down the street as far as I could see.

Just as I was beginning to contemplate what happened to

everyone, wondering if I was just dreaming, a car approached. It was a white four-door and it was headed toward me. Although I had never met Maggie before, nor would I know her car, I knew that it was her in that car. I knew we were the only two people in this incredible gap in time and that the Universe, Angelic Beings and all Divine Ones were intent on our meeting this day.

I floated the rest of the way to Maggie's. I felt guided and protected, but I had no idea why.

I hurried to the corner and turned right just in time to see Maggie getting out of the white car. As I looked beyond her, down her street, no one was there. Just Maggie and me.

I watched her walk up to her door, unlock it and go inside. Slowly, I finished my walk to her house, took a deep nervous breath and knocked on her door. The sound seemed to echo around the world in the stillness that had fallen. My ears were ringing with messages and stillness.

A woman with beautiful, crystal blue eyes and a softly rounded face answered the door. She smiled sweetly then opened the door wide.

"Come in. I am just needing to write something in my journal. Have a seat, please," she gestured to the sofa.

When Maggie finished writing she put down her journal and pen, then looked serenely around me. Her gaze seemed to focus above and beyond my physical body. I felt a tingling sensation on the crown of my head.

"I saw you just now, walking up the street," she said carefully gazing at something around my head.

"I thought that was you in the car," I said. "There was no one, absolutely no one on the streets on the way over here. It was sort of eerie, like everyone else fell off the planet. Or...it sort of felt like this meeting was meant to be — that everything in the universe was bringing it about." I hesitated, wondering if that sounded too weird.

Maggie looked directly into my eyes. "Yes. I know. I noticed something when I saw you walking. You were..."

She looked in another direction, as if someone had walked into the room. She seemed to be listening and then she said, "Well, never mind for now."

"What did you notice?" I wanted some sort of validation from her. I thought I knew what she was going to say. I felt like there were many angels carrying me there, but I wouldn't know for sure. How could I know? But Maggie kept a very tight-lipped look on her face, and I guessed she was listening to my guides.

"Let's talk about you and why you came to see me today."

"As I told you on the phone, I started getting massage a few months ago and all kinds of old issues have come up again. I thought I was over them and now I find myself crying over things from the past. Sometimes I think I'm losing my mind because I am also hearing things. I go places and hear things and look around and no one is speaking. Or someone talks to me and I hear more than the voice from their mouth...I'm not explaining this very well, am I?"

"You're doing a wonderful job. I understand. This massage work, do you know if the massage therapist is doing any type of energy work?"

"I'm not sure..." Suddenly I got a picture in my mind of a certificate on Stacie's wall. I had stared at it so many times when dressing and undressing but I didn't know what it meant...

"Is Reiki some type of energy work? Stacie, my massage therapist said she was going to cut back on the energy work. I wasn't sure what she meant by it."

"Yes, Reiki is a type of energy healing. This healing work you are receiving is helping you release old issues you have had buried, but as these past memories are released, sometimes you experience the old pain again. And the voices..."

Maggie looked around me again, as if she were checking with something beyond before answering, "I believe you have some psychic abilities that have long been hidden, or suppressed. The energy work is reawakening certain abilities within you."

I didn't say a word. I didn't think a thing. I didn't want to know.

But I did know. I'd always known.

Maggie asked me about the old issues. I shared with her dark secrets from my past. As we talked the depth of emotion that held me in my darkest hours seemed to lift and blow away. The issues disappeared as quickly as I shared them. The healing came in being able to share them. I was letting go and Maggie was giving me the space to do it. No judgments or analysis. Just pure, open, loving space.

My current issues, however, wouldn't blow away. All my latent abilities were causing friction in my otherwise normal existence.   How could I deal with hearing other people's thoughts?   How would I explain to my friends and family my conversations with angels and spirit guides?   Would I have to start wearing purple gauze skirts and carry a crystal ball?   It didn't suit my lifestyle.   I didn't think I was really cut out for the "psychic biz."

"I recently started learning Tarot. My mother thinks it's the devil's work," I looked at Maggie wondering. "She says all this stuff I'm reading and studying is just a fad. And my father, well, forget it. He doesn't want to know."

Maggie saw the difficulty I was having in accepting who I was because of the old beliefs from my family. Those beliefs were no longer serving me. I was ashamed and afraid to allow my gifts to surface.

"I think a past life regression would really help you see this in another light. I have a feeling there is old karma here you need to look at in order to move forward in this lifetime."

I shivered and looked into her eyes. My body was still quivering as I nodded in approval.

We planned on meeting in one week to take me back to another space and time.

As I walked home cars roared past, birds sang, children played and the earth was alive once more.

A few days after meeting with Maggie, Lauren and I were on our way to a video store when in my mind's eye I saw a car coming at top speed through the next intersection. As it approached my car on the driver's side, it raced through a stop sign and was going to pound into the side of the car, right where Lauren was in her car seat. It was a premonition – a warning – but I wasn't trusting my psychic flashes. I wasn't sure if I should trust them.

As I approached the cross street, I slowed down but continued into the intersection. The cross street had the stop sign, and I didn't trust the important message I had just received. I trusted that stop sign.

After entering the intersection, I looked to my left down the normally quiet street and the car from my vision was coming and it wasn't going to stop. I laid on the gas and flew through just in time. Just like in my vision, the car raced through the stop sign.

I was still shaking when we reached the video store. I walked in holding tightly to Lauren's hand. It was impossible to concentrate on the videos, so I wandered around the store hoping to shake my fright.

Then I ran into Maggie. She looked up from the videos as if she had been expecting me. I told her what had happened and she nodded and smiled knowingly.

"Spirit is going to teach you to trust your visions," she said simply and then she continued selecting her movies.

CHAPTER FIVE

AMBITION, ASSASSINATION, AND A SECOND CHANCE

The following week I sat in Maggie's den waiting for our session to begin. My stomach gurgled. I had been unable to keep food in my system all week. Toast and tea were all I could stomach for a full week.

"That's not surprising," Maggie had told me when I complained of my digestive problems. "The body remembers. It already knows what you will see today. It's good that you fasted. It is the natural way of healing and your body knew what to do. The fasting was a way of clearing your body so that you will remember your past more clearly."

She moved a few stones around into a circle on the table between us.

"Let's get started, shall we?" She motioned for me to lie back on the sofa. "You may want this." She pulled a blanket off the back of the couch and placed a pillow under my head.

Nerves were jumping inside me, so I appreciated her nurturing presence. I pulled the blanket up to my chin and clasped my hands tightly together underneath it.

Maggie smiled down on me. "Your body is ready. It has purged and prepared you for this journey. You are open and prepared internally to receive this information. It is all within you already. Today you shall begin to remember who you are."

Closing my eyes I took a deep breath in and shook the air back out. Then Maggie began to guide me.

"Take a deep breath in...there...now let it out very slowly. Now imagine with each breath that you are bringing in warm radiant light. Take another deep breath in and bring it all the way down into your toes. Allow your toes to relax."

I filled my toes with light and then my feet, ankles, calves, all the way up to the crown of my head. Maggie helped me to relax my entire body before inviting me to leave it behind. I felt completely serene.

"Now see yourself in a beautiful meadow...a beautiful green meadow. On a hill nearby you see a beautiful oak tree. Go to the tree and sit beneath it. Spend some time touching, feeling the tree. Feel the grass under you. Look at the blue sky. Listen to the birds singing."

I saw and felt every nuance of the picture as she painted it. The birds were there, the sun was warm on my face, the tree supported my back as I leaned against it. I was happily absorbed in the dream...

"Now I want you to follow the stone steps leading down the other side of the hill."

I didn't want to leave the safety of my oak tree. I felt safe and protected. And I was nervous about the past.

"Follow the steps down and soon you will hear a stream, and as you round the bend you see the stream as it flows alongside a small, worn path. Walk alongside the stream now, on the path."

Such a lovely stream it was! The water was crystal clear. I could see the stones at the bottom.

"You notice a leaf falling from the tree up on the hill. Your eyes follow the leaf as it gently descends into the stream. It is floating on the water. As it flows downstream follow it as you walk along the path."

Sure enough, just as Maggie said — the leaf was floating down the stream and I was following...

"There's a footbridge up ahead. You arrive there before the leaf and you walk up onto the bridge. Now stop in the middle and watch the leaf as it goes under the bridge."

I was so absorbed in following Maggie's instructions, I saw the leaf as it floated under the bridge, then suddenly my nerves were jumping inside of me again.

Uh-oh. I think I know where the bridge leads.

Maggie knew how to gently guide me across. Step by step she guided me, slowly and carefully she took me home, home to another life and time.

I felt so aware of everything here in this otherworldly place even though I hadn't stepped back in time yet. The stream was alive and the smells of the damp ground filled my nose. As I approached the other side of the bridge my body began to tremble. My eyelids flickered rapidly.

"As you step off the footbridge you will be in another time.'"

The ground was different here. Pine needles were under my feet. I felt new energy, the energy of another being. It felt both familiar and new.

Maggie no longer told me what to see but instead began asking many questions.

"Look at the ground under your feet. Can you describe it to me?"

"Yes. It is grassy. And there are pine needles. "

I was seeing things as if I were watching clips from a very old movie. The film flickered here and there and sometimes missed a beat. I was also in the film and as I moved, the scenery changed. I could look down at my hands and feet, and they were someone else's, but they were ME! I knew this being, I knew these hands! I remembered so many things all at once. The feelings were tremendous. As Maggie continued to ask me for information, I felt the answers come to me without any hesitation. It was all right there, I knew it.

"What else do you see?"

"I see lots of trees. There is a forest here."

"Can you tell me more about this forest? What kind of trees do you see? Do you know where you are?"

"It is very woodsy. Oh, it is very beautiful," I felt a deep love for the place where I lived. "Mostly I see evergreen trees. I am definitely in the mountains."

"Do you know where?"

"Colorado," came out without any thoughts. After I said it, I doubted my answer. I loved Colorado. Perhaps I said that because I wanted it to be Colorado. Or perhaps I loved Colorado because I lived there in another life. I pondered this for a second before Maggie asked me another question.

"I want you to look down at your feet. What do you see?"

I had already looked at my hands and feet and body. The first time I looked down, just on this side of the footbridge, my feet were barefoot, but now they had on moccasins. "I have moccasins on, I think." I tried to slow down the reel to reel film going by. If only my eyelids would quit fluttering! Looking at the rest of my body I see I am male and have long slender hands. They are very smooth and my skin is brown. My hair is long, black and in two thick braids. There is fringe down the arms of my clothing, which feels soft like deerskin.

"How old are you?" Maggie asks.

"I feel like I am in my twenties."

"Can you tell me your name?"

Doubt and hesitation grab me when I feel the name that first comes to me...I doubt it and don't want to say it out loud. While questioning the validity of my name, another name appears "Juniper..." as I say it I see myself as a young boy and realize this was a name I was given as a child, but there was another name I had later on...

The name Black Elk came to me first, but how could that be?

My name is Juniper. But that wasn't all.

"There was also a name like... Black Elk..." I hedged around wondering what Maggie was thinking. It was definitely 'Black Elk,' but I knew better. I must be imagining it; it's a name that's known, Jules. This is another ego trip. I can't believe I said it out loud!

"Now I want you to travel to your home. Tell me where you live."

There was a long pause before I followed her instructions. When I felt brave enough to move, there was no effort. My feet moved across the ground without touching it. As I approach our village I see the tepees and know how to get home. "I see our village. There are many, many tepees here."

"Go to yours and describe it to me."

I know which one it is and I stop outside the doorway. As I am standing still outside but saying nothing Maggie says "Go on inside." How did she know I wasn't moving?

I bend over to go through the opening in the canvas and then I let it close behind me. I breathe more deeply as my emotional body is becoming choked. Tears stream out the corners of my eyes and gravitate into my ears. My whole self feels overwhelmed with this homecoming.

MYSTIC MOMMY

I carefully sit down on the beautiful furs covering the floor. There is a tiny fire in the center of the tepee. Directly across from me are familiar faces. I look at the loving face of my wife and momentarily I see smiling faces of children. The tears continue to flow and I cannot find the words to describe my feelings.

"It's okay. Take a moment, then try to tell me how it feels." Maggie says to me very softly.

"It feels like home. I feel so good here. I have been searching for this place, this feeling...all of my life. I am so happy here." I stop talking and take it all in. I rub my hands on the furs and look at the loving faces. I feel at peace. I do not want to ever leave this place. I've found it. This is what I have been missing all my life — this life.

"Describe to me the other people here."

I gaze at the beautiful woman across from me. "My wife is very pretty. She has long hair. She holds a small child. I think there are other children. I can't see them all now, but I think they are here...outside the tepee." I see the children as they play outside. I sense how many are mine.

"Four. I have four children."

53

"You feel good with your family?" Maggie asks, but I know she is sensing what I am feeling.

"Yes, I have a lot of love for them." My heart is swelling with emotion for these people and this place. I wipe the tears from my cheeks with the tissue Maggie puts in my hands.

"Do you recognize any of these people from your current life?"

I begin to guess, but I am uncertain. The feelings I have for this soul who was my wife does not match with anyone I can immediately recall. I want it to be my husband in this life, but it doesn't feel the same. Two of my children feel like they could be Lauren and Grace. I look again at the faces of these children, "I'm not sure...maybe."

"That's all right. That may be clear to you later on. Now I want you to go about your day, see what it is you do."

Stepping out of the tepee I move about. I visit with other members of the tribe. I touch people a lot. As I stand listening to what someone is telling me, I also hear their thoughts and pick up on their feelings. And I always know what to say to help them heal.

"I can feel other peoples' burdens. I know everyone else's sorrows. I think I do some healing. I touch and reassure others."

"Are you a medicine man?"

My first sensation says, 'yes!' but I hesitate and doubt that could be true. Me? A medicine man?

"I am a wise person, but I am in training. I was born into a role, of a medicine person. It seems there was a knowing of who I was at my birth. But now I must wait. There is someone who is teaching me."

"How does the tribe feel about you?"

I am still moving about, having conversations that I cannot understand in a language I do not know. The feelings of the conversation cross over to me in the regression. I understand everything, although I do not know the words I say.

"Yes. I am loved. There are some though, who do not like what I say. I see things, of our future, and they do not always like what I share. My wife supports me. I share my feelings with her."

I see myself sitting alone on a high cliff wall. I am in a trance state and am receiving visions of the future. I see our tribe being slaughtered by the white man. I see the death and destruction that is coming. And as I try to share this with the tribe there is much anger and fear. They want things to stay the same and they do not want to hear what I am seeing.

My wife smiles gently as I step back into the tepee. Always she believes me. She supports me, loves me completely. It feels so strong, like a love I have yet to know.

I moved quickly back to the village and to Maggie's next instruction.

"I want you to go to the Medicine Man who is training you."

I walk to the end of a row of tepees right up to his. He sees me coming and is smiling knowingly. It is as if he can see and feel *everything*.

"Describe him to me."

"He's very tall, and very strong. He is older, I can see lines in his face. His demeanor is very strong."

MYSTIC MOMMY

"How do you feel around him? Are you comfortable?"

"No. I am not completely comfortable with him."

"Why? What can you tell me about your relationship with him?"

"I'm afraid to make a mistake. I feel like he judges me. He watches me and knows so much."

"How does he feel about you?"

I look into the face of this very wise man. I see his eyes smile at me. "He loves me." I tell Maggie, "I feel better standing here next to my mentor. It feels like I never before noticed his love for me. I was too fearful. He was very hard on me, but it was because he expected so much, and knew I was capable. He wanted me to step into my power position, but I hid behind him and his abilities."

"I would like you to go to the time just before your death and describe it to me."

I feel my body quiver more intensely.

"It's all right. We can go slowly." Maggie sensed my sudden fright.

57

I tried to describe what I was seeing and experiencing to Maggie, but my voice was breaking up. "I am sleeping in my tepee and I wake up because of voices yelling and shouting. There is fighting somewhere. Everyone is getting on horses. I see people being killed." I stop, because I see Juniper having visions again of people being killed. I realize these are his visions, not what is happening.

"Go on. What do you do?"

I feel myself frozen in time. I do not want to leave with the others. Everyone is leaving, at least all the men. I don't want to leave. My body shakes uncontrollably now and I cannot speak.

"It's okay. You're safe. Let's just move very slowly. What are you doing and how do you feel?" Maggie asks me very patiently. I want to respond, but my body is fighting against an uncontrollable outburst of emotion.

"I—I—I—don't want to go!" I sob.

"What are you doing?"

"I'm with my family. We are huddled together in the tepee. I don't want to leave. I'm afraid."

"Okay. You must move forward now. What do you do?"

"I am getting on my horse. I know I must help — I must fight. I am riding into the woods..."an overwhelming feeling comes over me, "I don't feel afraid anymore." I tell Maggie and then breathe easily. My sobbing has stopped.

"What do you see now? Where are you?"

"I see everyone returning to the village. It was a false alarm. There was a mistake...oh..."I suddenly realize I am watching from above. I see everyone gathered around my body.

"You need to go back. We need to go back to the time of your death. You moved past that." Maggie seems to be in a hurry to gather me back. I feel something pulling me upward. I feel so good I want to go with the feeling. I am moving into a peaceful place of pure white light. I no longer see the tribe nor feel anything but peace.

"Juli, I need you to come back. I want you to go to when you first get on the horse."

Maggie's firm command must be for a good reason, although I wish I could follow the white light...I have never felt so at peace. I listen to Maggie and am riding into the woods once more. "I am the last to leave. Everyone else has gone ahead." I feel pain in my left ear all at once. "I think I fell off my horse. I feel pain in my left ear." I feel blood coming out of my head, or my ear. I know there is a great deal of blood. Again I feel myself moving into the space of light and peace.

"No, wait. We aren't finished here. Come back. Just before you hit your head."

What is Maggie trying to accomplish? I hit my head, died, now would she let me go on into that blissful feeling I was beginning to experience!

Wait... I hit my head on a rock when I fell, but how did Maggie know that? Did I mention it?

I oblige her and once more I am on my horse. This time I am moving so slowly. Everything is in slow motion and I sense someone is behind me. Then I feel something else, another pain, the something that sent me off of my horse...

"I've been shot! Someone shot me in the back! An arrow has gone through my heart!" I am filled with anger, intense anger...I can't believe it! "I feel like someone did all this...I have been...betrayed."

Maggie lets out a heavy sigh, "Yes. Okay. You may move through your death now. But I want you to stick around. Watch from above, if need be, but see what happens after your death. Do you know who killed you...and why?"

From above I see everyone come to my side after discovering my body, "My family is very upset. I see my wife. She is crying and so are others. But ...there is someone standing back aways. This person is not sad." I look more closely at the one hiding in the distance, watching, "It is my brother. He is not sorry that I died."

"Why?"

"He was jealous of my talents. I knew something was going to happen to the tribe. He did not like my talk of these things. I saw the coming of the white man and the killing that would follow. I tried to warn everyone, but not everyone wanted to hear it. My brother encouraged others not to listen to me. He wanted me out of his way. He never received the same respect and always felt as if he was living in my shadow."

"Did he kill you?"

"I am not sure. I don't think he shot the arrow." I feel

sorrow for my family, "I want to go back, to comfort my family."

"What do you see happening?"

"I see my mentor touching my wife." I feel a pit in my stomach.

"How does that make you feel?"

"Angry. I am jealous that he can touch her."

"What else? What about your brother?"

"I see him talking with some others. They are back by the trees, away from the tribe, my brother and two others who knew of my death. I feel it was planned."

Maggie allows me to breathe through these feelings a moment. "I want you to come back now and you will have a chance to talk with Juniper." She guides me back to my own self but stops me on the footbridge and invites Juniper to come and talk to me.

We meet in the middle.

"What does Juniper want you to know? What was the

purpose of this life?"

I am standing close to him. I feel such love for him. I also feel a lot of regret for his life being cut short. He speaks to me in fragments and through feelings. I try to relay the meaning to Maggie, "He says it was to help others, in a spiritual way. He wanted to help but couldn't do enough due to his death. He knew so much but he did not have enough time to share his knowledge. He learned about love and family, and how important these things are. He felt he had so much in that regard, that it made it possible to help others. He had love and support within his family, but his purpose was to share what he had with the others."

"Does he have regrets he wishes to share with you?"

I barely hear Maggie's question as Juniper is filling me with information. I answer her question as Juniper continues to dialogue with me, "he regrets that he was afraid to say things. He kept quiet and was waiting for the right time. He feels he should have spoken."

"What does he advise you to do?"

Maggie asks me the question after Juniper has given me the answer, "He says, 'Trust yourself. You know so much more than you allow yourself. Quit denying your wisdom.

Don't remain quiet. Don't hide what you know.'"

He's laughing now, he is telling me funny things. We are having a great time, like two old friends. I share some of it with Maggie, "He says, 'Don't be so serious. You need to laugh more.'" Juniper knows me well.

"Can he instruct you on how to remove the obstacles in your current life?"

"Yes. He says to forgive. I must forgive my brother, first of all."

"Is there anything else he wants you to know?"

"Yes." I listen as he speaks, again, I receive his language through feelings. "He is telling me to use my gifts, to help others and to not be fearful."

Juniper and I hug and say good-bye. As we embrace he melds into my being and then I see him float out through the top of my head. He floats up and out of my sight. I am standing on the footbridge alone, watching a leaf float gently down the stream.

"Very good. Now follow the path back up the stream..." Maggie brings me back up the steps to the oak tree and slowly she helps me focus my attention on my physical body and the room. I remain lying down and pull the blanket up close to me.

After a few moments, Maggie speaks, very softly at first.

"It felt very strong, your death scene. It was of major importance, which is hard to describe. It felt like an historical assassination. I knew right away it was planned."

"You did? You could see it?" I sat up on the sofa and looked closely into her eyes as she spoke. She spoke as she looked off into the air...

"I saw everything. Before you said 'Colorado' I knew it was Colorado."

"Really? Were you there?"

"I wasn't alive, but I was there. I felt very connected to you, like a grandmother. Definitely someone who had passed over already, but I was there to watch over you."

I sat staring at Maggie. I was overwhelmed by everything I saw and felt. I felt homesick. I wanted to go back. It was real, and now I understood my strong connection with Maggie. I was glad she was there, and could witness what I saw.

"Oh, and there was someone else that was with you." Maggie was getting up and I guessed she had another appointment coming soon. I didn't want to go back out into the world just yet. I wanted to integrate all I saw and heard and felt. I wanted to be with Juniper.

I began to wonder how real it could have been. While experiencing it **I knew it was real**. But now I couldn't imagine what I would tell my family and my fear filled me with doubt.

"Yes, at the end, a spirit guide was there and wanted me to let you know he is with you. He was very tall and his name is..."I saw her looking over me again and listening to the other side, "Longfellow."

I looked into her eyes. How does she know these things? How did she know I needed validation right then? Or did Longfellow know I need to know what is true? Longfellow. He appeared to me during my massage with Stacie.

Maggie guided me to the door. After she closed it behind me I stood alone on the stoop. Then I remembered Longfellow...I guess I'm not alone.

I walked home no longer ignoring the spirit guide near me.

"Black Elk."

Longfellow was speaking directly to me. A chortle came out my nostrils, "yeah, right." I snidely remarked back to this entity as if I were talking to my ego.

"Black Elk."

"What are you trying to tell me? Black Elk! Black Elk is so famous and I'm sure everyone who thinks they were him is probably . . ."

"Black Elk was a name, a family name. Not the name of one man. You were an ancestor . . . "

Is that possible? I was beginning to wonder if the whole thing was made up by me, because of my love for all things Native...or do I love all things Native because I was once...?

My love of the Native American culture since I was a young girl was suddenly crystal clear. I always felt that was my true heritage, not the German-Lutheran background of my birth family. Now I understood.

I had been longing for home and to be a part of a family that existed in another lifetime. I longed for what Juniper had — the love of his family, peace and contentment for what is and an understanding of his role in the community. His gifts had been recognized at his birth. His only regret: that he wasn't able to share more of what he knew.

And what I felt while in Juniper's moccasins felt more real than this — more real than the sidewalk I was walking on. The needles on the pine trees back in Colorado, back there, back then, were more vibrant than the leaves on these oaks. And the love I felt for my wife and children, for our tepee, for the earth, it filled my heart until it felt like it would burst open and...

Then I felt the anger, and I recognized the characters repeating in this lifetime. I knew the pain in my heart in this lifetime was because of those who could not accept my gifts, then and now, myself included. The same lessons were repeating in this lifetime.

"It's just a dream." I still hear them saying.

All through my childhood, the dreams that I felt were so significant were not valued.

"It's just your imagination!" others would tease.

MYSTIC MOMMY

Was I going to let my fear stop me again? Would I continue to lead my life based on others' expectations and beliefs?

I had to move past the fear. Would I really share my wisdom this time?

After meeting Juniper I felt compassion for him. I wanted to succeed for him. Even if I die trying, I thought, at least I'll try.

CHAPTER SIX

QUANDARY MOUNTAIN

Dreamtime: *I am sitting at the edge of a cave with my legs dangling over a rocky precipice. I don't want to look down. An inconceivable distance hangs below me. Instead I look out toward the surrounding mountains, but I am unable to enjoy the view because of a tremendous fear.*

Sitting close behind me is a creature of great power, courage and strength. Too frightened to turn around, I remain paralyzed. I know what it is...back there...behind me...in the cave. Of course I'm not going to turn around— I can't face her. Not here, especially not on this rocky ledge.

Cat RunningElk

But I know the mountain lion in that cave is looking at me...

Ted finished up his Masters degree and was ready to start his new career somewhere other than our hometown. We were both longing to go out West. I had lived in Colorado before I married Ted and I still missed the Rocky Mountains. After seeing my lifetime as Juniper I understood why I loved Colorado so much.

My guides wanted us to go to the Pacific Northwest, but Ted and I weren't ready to move that far away. We had friends in Colorado and I was anxious to return to what felt like my spiritual home.

We left in our used Range Rover and pulled a U-Haul trailer behind us. Grace's final adoption proceedings were that same day. We closed on our house, went to the courthouse and finalized the adoption, then headed for Colorado.

The Range Rover began leaking oil just after we got out of Cedar Rapids. We stopped in the next town and were told we would need major repairs. Not wanting to turn around, we bought a case of oil. The back window became covered with black oil and we kept putting more oil in the engine. Soon we couldn't see what we'd left behind.

We arrived in Boulder and moved into a house our friends had found for us. I could *see* the mountains out my front window, but I longed to be *in* them.

We drove up into the mountains a little further each outing. The day we drove three hours from Boulder and found ourselves sitting on top of the world, high in Summit County, we knew we were home.

The prices on homes were as steep as the mountains that surrounded them. But I knew my guides would help us. I knew we were almost home.

Our realtor called us up one day and said, "I've got it. The owner is willing to do an owner carry mortgage and it has the three bedrooms and great views, everything you wanted."

We took it.

Our new home was on Quandary Mountain calmly sitting at over eleven thousand feet. The Continental Divide stood majestically on one side of our home and out my living room window was North Star Mountain. For the next year these mountains seemed to guide me to the answers I was seeking.

My visions became as clear as the mountain air. They came easily and often. And always in my dreams, that mountain lion was watching.

Then one night she wasn't there. The mountain lion that had been back there, behind me, was gone. The cave was empty. I was afraid for I knew she was out there, somewhere, waiting for me.

CHAPTER SEVEN

HAVEN'T WE MET BEFORE?

A young woman parks her car at the grocery and helps her two small children out. She carries a small, dark-skinned girl not much more than a year old on her hip. The other child, a three-year-old girl with fair skin and blonde hair is taken by the hand as they head to the entrance. The woman stops outside the grocery store to peruse the community bulletin board. She thinks it is another insignificant moment in another insignificant day.

The hidden camera zooms in on a piece of paper hanging on the bulletin board. A large rainbow covers the background of the paper. It ruffles in the breeze catching *the woman's attention. "Reiki I and II Classes and a Group Past Life Regression..."*

Fumbling in her purse for a pen and paper she puts down the child she carries and releases the hand of the other. She is writing the phone number...

It was time to remember once again who I am... and why I have come.

I was introduced to Trevor before the others. He had flown in from Boston for the weekend to be initiated to the second degree of Reiki with Elaine, the Reiki Master and Teacher. This evening we would all be experiencing a group past life regression. The following day our Reiki initiation would begin.

Trevor and I looked at one another for more than a moment as we shook hands and exchanged social pleasantries. It was a typical, "haven't we met before?" type of feeling. I wasn't about to appear flirtatious, so I resisted the desire to say it.

Trevor also seemed to hold back words, and we let our hands drop awkwardly. I didn't notice anyone else because after looking into his eyes all I could think about was where we'd met before. How did I know him? Something about him was so familiar.

As our teacher and guide introduced me to the others I barely heard their names. I gave everyone a polite hello and a warm handshake, and then found a comfortable place to sit on the floor with my back leaning against the sofa. After I sat, Trevor came and sat on the sofa directly behind me and the others assembled around us.

Elaine introduced herself to all of us again, "Hi. I'm Elaine. I'm a Reiki Master and I'm here this weekend teaching Reiki One and Two to many of you in this room. I've had some really wonderful experiences healing others with Reiki and using past-life meditations. So I thought I would lead a group past-life regression for all of you. Obviously you all have some belief or curiosity about past lives or you wouldn't have responded to the flyer I posted at the grocery store."

I remembered calling about the Reiki class when I saw the ad with the rainbow in the background. Back in Iowa I had participated in healing circles at Maggie's for several months. That alone seemed to awaken some sort of healing ability within me.

Then one night meditating I saw an angel touch my hands. In that moment I began to feel a pulsating energy in my palms when I was around certain people. It made me want to put my hands on them, which is what the angel told me to do, "Just touch people," she said.

Now I wanted some external validation. I wanted to receive the Reiki training so that I could be a real healer, a certified healer.

And the experience of stepping into another life and time was so profound and so healing, I wanted to know more. I felt I could help others by learning more about how to guide them into their past lives...

Elaine's Boston accent drew me back into the group, "I want you to get a sense of what it is like..."

She went on about past life regressions while my mind chatter continued...

I already know how to do this. I've done so many of these before. Why am I here, really?

I tried to ignore my egotistical voice –

I'm here because I want to learn more and see how another person does it. I plan on teaching past-life regression to others someday. It will be good to get a broader perspective on how it's done.

As Elaine gave us general instructions my mind continued to judge how she was doing it. I compared everything to the way my previous teacher had led me through past-life regressions.

"Now close your eyes. Take a deep breath and let it out very slowly..."

Elaine paused as we began to exhale nervous tension, stress, worries and pain. "Another long, slow breath in...Hold it!...Okay, let it out... Imagine a rope tied around your waist. It is connected to the earth and will protect your body while we travel."

I remembered how my other teacher led me into past lives...*What is this rope for? Maggie didn't need any rope to keep me safe. How silly.*

"With your next in-breath feel yourself expanding. The energy fills your entire being and now you are expanding in size with each breath. Notice how large your hands are, feel your right hand, it is the size of a football..."

This is ridiculous! Sure my hand feels like it is the size of a football. But why? When is she going to lead us to the path next to the stream? I really liked the way Maggie did this with the nice little bridge that led us from this lifetime into the others...

"Now breathe in again and notice how your other hand is the size of a football..."

Elaine's voice was calm and relaxed.

I impatiently awaited further directions. My mind was qualifying me as an expert now even though I had only done this a few times before. For some reason I was extremely judgmental and not open to a new teacher and new experiences.

Perhaps it was really nervousness in disguise. I had already learned that fear accompanies the realization of truth, especially truth that has remained carefully hidden for years.

I didn't expect to realize any great hidden truth about myself. I only hoped to pick up a few tips from this spiritual teacher with the quiet voice and heavy East Coast accent.

Elaine had a certain wisdom about her. She presented herself as a calm, gentle spirit. She was ageless, somewhere over forty with silver hair that revealed nothing of age but everything of her true essence — wisdom.

"Your whole body is now as big as this room," Elaine continued. "With your next breath you expand beyond these walls. You are growing out and beyond the confines of this house. You will now find the bigger you become, the lighter you are, rising up above the house into the night sky..."

I found myself already up in the stars, well above the earth. Looking back down, the universe stood still, just for a moment...

"Now lift up higher and higher. A cloud comes by and gently picks you up. It carries you farther and farther into the sky and up to the edge of the Earth's atmosphere..."

Whoops! I didn't know about the cloud thing! I raced back to earth to await my cloud ride. Swiftly the cloud carried me back out — way out. Looking back at earth again I saw it turn and then stop. After an instant it turned the other way and I descended back to earth. Was time moving in reverse as the earth's rotation changed? Or was it my imagination?

Elaine was catching up to me. "As you are leaving earth's atmosphere keep floating gently up into the stars..."

I no longer questioned my ability to go ahead of Elaine's directions. My intuition was leading me on.

"Notice the planets near you and far away. As you look back down at the Earth notice how it is rotating. Now it stops...just for an instant. As you come back down toward the Earth you see it begin to rotate in the opposite direction..."

As Elaine guided everyone else back to earth, I was ready to land. My spirit hovered above the earth...anxiously awaiting her directions. For some odd reason I was hesitant again. I felt afraid to step into this alternate life and time without her guidance.

"As you come closer and closer to the earth you recognize the continents. As you come closer and closer you will ascertain where you are going..."

I already knew I was hovering above Africa. I could point to the area on a map, but there was no grid, no cities, villages or towns. As I came in for a landing all I saw were huts, skinny cows, and people – tribal people. Still hovering above the dusty ground I awaited my teacher's instructions.

Come on, come on, Elaine. I can't wait up here forever.

MYSTIC MOMMY

"You are noticing the topography of this part of the world. Gently come in closer and closer to the Earth..."

I couldn't stand it. My feet touched the ground without my teacher's directions. My impatience overcame my fear.

The air was hot and dry and the ground under my feet was dry and dusty. Looking down I saw the dark skin of my feet. Twine was twisted around my ankles and down between my toes like sandal straps, more decorative than functional.

I moved my attention up my body and I saw a colorful sarong wrapped around my legs and tied at the waist. The skirt clung to my body as did a young child at my side. A small baby rested in my arms. Row after row of beaded jewelry hung heavily on my neck. There was no clothing on my upper body, just ever widening circles of necklaces. Up and down my arms were bracelets, many of them cuff bracelets that tightly clutched the bones of my arms. My earlobes were heavily weighted with more beaded metal rings.

For a moment I stepped out of the woman I was and I looked directly at her...at me. My black hair was shaved close to my head and my jaw line was strong and severe. My thin face was accented by high cheekbones and penetrating eyes.   I looked severe and serious. A weight heavier than the jewelry and children seemed to hang on me.

My eyes were hauntingly deep but they had a magnetic quality that pulled me in.   The color eluded me.   It was beyond any color of the earth.   Within my eyes I saw the earth and everything on it.   When I tried to look at the eyes alone, they disappeared and I saw the universe.

A memory came rushing back.   I remembered that this woman had come to me in a dream.   She had a message. What had she been trying to tell me?   Now I saw that I was her.

I remembered it was just before Grace arrived home from India that this woman appeared to me in a dream. She had a child in her arms and one at her side, as she did here.

In my dream she also had many children all around her. She was walking down a path, people before her and others following behind her. Although there were many others, my focus and attention remained on her.   She seemed to be telling me something.   In her eyes I sensed a warning. Deeply into mine she had gazed long and hard. She had the look and feel of an earth mother, and I wondered at the time if she was the Mother of All Mothers come to me to give me advice and strength as I anxiously awaited the arrival of my second child. But her eyes looked into me and left me feeling afraid, perhaps not afraid, but definitely a bit intimidated.

At the time of that vision I felt blessed to have seen and met her. I hoped to be as wonderful a mother as I sensed she was.

And now, she and I were one.

Elaine directed us to move forward in the regression a few years. I saw my life several years later, and I stood the same as before, but now there were three children. A babe at my breast, a child as tall as my hip who clung to my skirt, and another up to my waist.

We moved forward again a few years and I saw the same scene; a baby in my arms, one at my skirt and the others growing up next to me. A feeling of futility washed over me. I was not the great earth mother with messages of how to be a wonderful, perfect mother. I was a mother frustrated with what my role in life was to be. This woman I was had great love for her children, but within her was also a yearning for something more.

Time passed like the fading in and out of a movie scene.

Always I had a child in my arms and one at my side and older ones playing nearby. The addition of children revealed the passage of years.

I knew that I was the daughter of the chief of this tribe. Our village had no name. We were concerned only with our own existence and cared nothing for the world beyond our village. All that mattered was the here and now.

I felt the power within me to heal and to receive information from the spirit world. I gave the credit to my birthright and anticipated a time when I could utilize my gifts. But I didn't share my gifts now. It wasn't my place.

As I met and greeted other members of our village I picked up on their thoughts and understood their needs for healing. But I kept my thoughts to myself and I healed no one. It was not my place to heal or speak of my abilities. It was only for my father to do these things.

My father served the tribe well. He visited with most everyone every day and made certain their needs were met. Following my father around I saw all that he did. I wanted to help, but I felt I couldn't. The healing was my father's job.

My father and I locked eyes and communicated without

words. He understood my abilities but would not allow me to show others what I could do as a healer, a wise woman and a sage. Without speaking he said I must wait.

I am told to wait. Again and again I am told simply to wait. Silently I watched as time faded in and out over many more years, and still I waited.

After some time he stopped looking at me and then eventually he avoided my stare altogether. I knew he didn't want me to read his thoughts. He was afraid of how much I knew. It felt as though I could intimidate him.

And yet I waited for his approval.

As a new scene appears I sensed it was time for my father to die. He looked at me and then at the children and communicated without words that it was time for him to go.

Without mournful good-byes he prepared to leave. It would simply be a passing into another place, another dimension. My father was aware that his passing was merely a release of his spirit — something one can choose if one is spiritually advanced, like he was. And so he prepared to be released.

He walked into his hut and lay down on the bed.

Through a window over the bed he stared into the sky. I knew he would soon leave his body. I wanted to speak with him one last time, but out of respect I remained silent and waited to see the outcome of his passing, for after his spirit was free he would choose.

His spirit would choose the next Chief. This was the way the next chief was always chosen. The next in line would soon be blessed. It felt as though I had been waiting my whole life for this moment. I was ready to be the chosen one.

In the light of the full moon I saw my father's spirit floating above the hut. He had left his body. As I closed my eyes my body stiffened, but nothing happened.

I opened my eyes just in time to see my father's spirit blessing my husband. He didn't come near me. After passing through my husband his spirit moved on into an unseen world and he never looked back.

My eyes wide I looked at my husband. He had felt the chill of my father's blessing. He looked into my eyes for a moment. My father's power and position was now my husband's.

I was furious. Flames of anger flashed out of my eyes. I

glared at my husband and he quickly turned away. He turned to face the village and his duty.

So began his reign.

CHAPTER EIGHT

BECOMING CHIEF

The night my father died faded into darkness. A new day arose and I was ever the mother figure. There was a child at my breast and one clutching my skirt. Older children gathered around me — some were mine and there were many more who were not my biological children.

Many of the children in the tribe came to me for caring or special herbs or advice. It was part of my role as the chief's wife to attend to the children. Other adults worked hard all day farming, cooking or beading, but my duties were for the children.

My husband now carried the tall staff my father once carried. He was a good chief and a good medicine man. He conversed with the elders for advice and heard their stories. He gave remedies to all who needed healing. He worked with those who quarreled to make peace. He made sure there was always enough food for the tribe.

I was not happy in my role and I blamed him. My gifts were not recognized and the Chief, my husband, knew it. What could be done? I had looked first to my father for permission to share what I had inside and after his death I looked to my husband for the same approval. I was still waiting.

He sat on the cot in our hut as I stood near the doorway. I could not hear dialogue, but we were communicating. There was no peace for us. Our communication was always filled with my pain.

So instead we focused on our responsibilities, mine to the children and his to the village.

I knew I could work with others in resolving differences and keeping peace. I knew I could help with the healing work. But he said no — it wasn't for me to do. There was no way for us to work together.

Mystic Mommy

What bothered me the most was that he wouldn't even look at me. How could he not allow me to do what had been my birthright? Why did my father choose him and not me?

I wished I could make him understand. I needed to use my gifts. I was dying inside.

I decided to teach my children all that I knew. All the healing I learned from my father and from my grandmother I would share with my daughters and sons alike. The children already knew the stories of the earth and the moon and of the ancient ones before us and the star people. I had been sharing these stories with them since they were very young.

I heard Elaine's voice giving us another direction to move forward.

Immediately I went to my home, children always in tow and running beside me. Stopping in the open doorway I saw our simple dwelling, the cot, the open window and the dirt floor. I looked for my husband, but our hut was empty.

My husband had gone and the entire village was in an uproar. A terrible drought was upon us and I did not know where he was.

"When will your husband be back?" the villagers asked me whenever they saw me.

"Where is he? I need some healing!" I wanted to help them but I believed they didn't trust me.

"We need rain! Where has he gone? There is much sickness...we need him!" They were angry and scared. I told them I was certain he was doing what he knew would bring the rain to heal the land.

But I wondered why he had been gone so long.

I continued to shrug my shoulders when they asked me their questions. I felt certain no one wanted my help, so I didn't even try.

With my youngest on my hip, I walked back to our hut. "Where is he?" I wondered to myself. The land was desperately dry and nothing would grow. We needed the rain.

Why did he go now? I knew he would not desert us, but he did not tell me he was leaving. I didn't know what to say to the people.

During dry spells we usually prayed and danced together

as a community, but this time he had left. With only his staff he had left and now the days were drifting by.

The cattle were thin and sick. We all knew that if the rain did not come soon the cattle would die. We needed the cattle and the cattle needed the grass and the grass needed the rain.

I knew my husband was filled with magical powers, and I knew he would succeed in bringing us the rain. I hoped it would be soon.

I stood in the open doorway gazing out across the plain. If only the people would allow me to help. I felt useless not being allowed to use my powers.

I turned inward and an apparition of my father and my husband appeared on the cot in our hut. They were laughing at me. I stared at my competition. Resentment filled my being and I wondered why these wise men wouldn't allow me to use my gifts and powers. I wanted them to *give me my freedom — to allow me to use my gifts*. I blamed them both for my frustration.

Suddenly clouds moved across the sky and the sun disappeared making everything in the room appear gray. Thunder clouds crashed and the sound awakened me and erased the apparitions of my husband and father. The sound of raindrops magically filled the emptiness left behind.

Just as the rain began, my husband appeared in the doorway. He stood there a moment leaning heavily on his staff, which towered over his small, stooped frame. He then moved his thin body carefully to the cot and laid down upon it.

Rain was thundering on the roof now. Whoops and hollers from children and adults alike echoed into our hut through the window and doorway.

I turned back from the joy outside to look at my husband. I knew he had brought the rain. I wanted to find out where he had gone and what he had done, but whatever he did to bring the rain had exhausted him. His eyes were closed and he was breathing very slowly.

I stood watching and waiting. I had never seen him this way. He was smaller now than I remembered. His breathing was almost at a standstill.

I quickly called the oldest children to come. By the look on my face they knew what was happening.

We gathered around and he left quickly.

MYSTIC MOMMY

Just like when my father died I saw my husband's spirit as it left his body. The moon shone in the window over the bed. My husband, the chief, lay still on the same cot where my father died.

I was astonished to feel his spirit gently touch and bless me. I felt him smile at me as he went. He had given me permission to share my abilities. Now I had the power that was my husband's, and before that my father's. I finally felt free to be all I could be.

After his death it felt like my life began.

I was the medicine woman for the tribe now. I was their chief.

CHAPTER NINE

THE TRUTH IS REVEALED

Word of my husband's death traveled quickly. His parting gift of rain was welcomed and no one else but me wondered how he had brought it or why he had to die so soon afterward. I found myself thinking that I might have been able to heal him if only there had been more time...

Confidently I made my rounds to care for the village. I was surprised that everyone accepted my new position. Was it only my own doubts and insecurities that stopped me before? The blessing of my husband allowed me to be who I was. Did anyone else ever doubt that this was what I was meant to do? And how could he have stopped me from being who I was meant to be?

Memories of my father and my husband seemed unreal, like an illusion to teach me about my own power that had always been there, within me. I had been caught up in the illusion of believing someone else could keep my power from me, but I saw them laughing with me now.

I started out doing my work with a baby on my hip and other children following close behind, but soon other women offered to care for my youngest ones.

"Here, let me take care of them today."

My youngest was lifted from my hip, and I turned and saw my sister smiling at me. She hugged my child close to her bosom. I felt content knowing that the children were all loved and cared for and I went on to care for the elderly and sick, to settle disputes and to manage the cattle.

I enjoyed this scene. I felt powerful and appreciated. Everyone talked lovingly of the things my husband did for them as they reached out their hands and welcomed me into their homes.

I listened to them as I tended to their needs. I was listening to them tell stories over and over again of the rain coming when Elaine's voice said, "Go to the time of your death."

I swirled and spun out of control for a moment, and then found my focus in the starry night sky. I leaned on the same staff my husband and my father used during their reigns. Using it to support my elderly bent form, I stepped into my hut. It was time. It felt right even though I was neither ill nor unable to function in my physical body. I just knew it was my time.

Something, or someone, was calling me home.

I reflected on the many years I was the chief. I lived a long life and I healed and counseled many. Contentment and peace filled me as I remembered the love and respect that I felt for myself and that I received from the villagers. Using my abilities gave me the greatest feeling I had ever known.

My children and grandchildren gathered around me as I sat on the hard cot under the open window. I talked with all of them and said good-bye and then all but two of my children left me. My oldest daughter and son remained at my side. I lay on the same raised bed under the same open window where I saw my father and husband die.

Outside the window the full moon smiled down on me. I felt as though the moon was speaking to me — as if she was the one calling me home.

Smiling back at the moon, I closed my eyes. A rushing sensation liberated me. No longer in my body I gently rose into the night sky.

Looking back down I saw my children and instantly focused on my eldest daughter. I felt my spirit pass through her. Tearfully she reached up toward me. I passed my blessing on to my daughter, but her own power would carry her forward.

There would be mixed feelings in the tribe about having another woman as chief. What would happen was not for me to know, but I did know I had chosen well. My daughter was strong. She would do well.

I smiled down upon her and upon my eldest son, whom I also loved. "It is for you to continue, to lead the tribe." My spirit said to them, "I am going..."

Turning towards the moon I began to move upward.

"Now return to an awareness of your body in this room." Elaine interrupted my peaceful merging into the cosmos. I wanted to enjoy my ascent, but she directed us to return to the here and now. Carefully she guided us back up, onto our clouds and then once again to the Earth, to Colorado and into the room.

Hesitantly I came back into Juli's form. I looked at my hands and feet and barely recognized them. My heart was racing and my palms were sweaty.

How much time had passed?

Elaine asked us to each share our experiences with the group.

My insecurities began nipping at my heels again. *I can't share what I think I saw.* What had been so real a moment ago was fading and my doubts were surfacing. *It is so ridiculous and so obviously an ego trip. My imagination must be controlled by my incredible ego!* I tried to listen to the others as the stories began, but I could barely hear over my inner voices.

"I was riding a beautiful white horse through a field and..."

See how nice her story is? My inner critic continued to tear me apart. *Yours will sound ridiculous!*

"I didn't get anywhere..."

Huh? My mind suddenly quieted and I turned to listen to a man lamenting that he had experienced nothing. How could someone not see anything? My imagination goes wild with images every time I close my eyes. What had he been doing all this time? I tried to hide my appalled look.

"No. Nothing." He reiterated.

He and Elaine talked a bit and he agreed to try it again later with just Elaine.

"Juli, what about you?"

"Umm, well..." I was so nervous that my voice was cracking. I looked down at the floor and picked at the carpet with my fingers.

"I was living in Africa, I think..."

"Okay, can you describe what you looked like?" Elaine tried to help me along.

"Ummm, well, yes, I think I was a native woman, and I wore, um," I was looking at my arms and remembering in visions exactly what I looked like.   "They were like armbands, no, more like cuff bracelets on my arms, and I have on a sarong skirt thing and..." I was reliving it as I spoke. My voice picked up speed as all the images came flying through my mind.

"I have children. Well, in the beginning maybe two, one hanging on to my skirt and one in my arms. Then you said to jump forward in time and I have two more, one at my skirt and one in my arms again, plus the first two are just taller now." The more I spoke, the more real it felt.

"I am the chief's daughter; at least I think so, in the beginning. It is very frustrating to me because he won't let me do any of the healing work and ..." My entire being was shaking uncontrollably. I hoped no one noticed. All I could do was surrender to the story flowing out of my mouth.

"When he dies he gives his power to my husband. I just can't believe it! Why didn't he pick me?" I looked up into Elaine's eyes to see if she understood. I was furious with the men in this past lifetime. Did she see the injustice in all of this?

"I try to speak to the chief, my husband. We are in this hut. It has no real windows, just an opening over the bed and an opening that is rather short for a doorway, and just this one bed. He is sitting there and I am trying to ask him why I can't..."

Suddenly Trevor leapt to his feet from behind me and looked down at me as I crouched on the floor. Waving his arms frantically he spoke in a loud voice focused only on me.

"And you are standing there looking at me with those eyes! You had the most intense eyes!"

I sat open-mouthed with a question on my face.

"You could look right through me!" Trevor seemed to shudder as he remembered the look.

Silently I questioned him and he read my mind and continued...

"Yes. Oh my God! I was there! I was HIM! The chief! I was your husband!"

I looked around the room for one frightening instance to see if I was dreaming. Everyone sat with jaws dropped staring at Trevor and me.

"You would give me these looks all the time. I knew you were angry with me, but I went on doing what needed to be done."

MYSTIC MOMMY

Now I remembered as if I were the African Woman again and had just been given the opportunity of a lifetime, of many lifetimes. My dead husband was back, standing in front of me. Now I could find out what I had wanted to know before.

"Where did you go? We needed the rain so badly. But you were gone so long and then..."

This was part of my story I had not yet shared with the group. Yet Trevor was there, and he knew exactly what I was talking about. Of course HE knew. This was the mission of his life and it cost him his...

Trevor and I felt ourselves swept away from the rest of the room as we filled in the blanks for each other. As he shared his experience with me, I saw everything that had happened...

"We needed rain so badly, I knew we wouldn't make it if I didn't do something desperate. I had my staff..."

"Yes, I remember the staff and how you wielded it even though you were quite..."

"Short. I know. But I had that tall staff and I walked and walked for days...."

"Everyone wanted to know where you went. I didn't know what to tell them..."

"I didn't know either. I just knew I had to go and do something. Something spurred me on, kept me going, 'til I reached a tall mountain. There were thunderclouds nearby so I climbed to the highest peak on that mountain."

With his whole body Trevor reenacted the deliberate steps he took to reach the summit. I was only aware of him and could no longer see anyone else in the room.

"When I finally reached the top I put all the power I could raise, more than I had ever found in me before, and I raised the staff high overhead and reached into the thunderclouds..."

Trevor stood over me like Goliath now, his massive presence reaching up over his head with an invisible staff.

"And I connected with those thunderclouds."

I believed his story and mine. They fit together and it made sense to me. Impossible, yet so real.

"I dragged those clouds all the way back to the village. I traveled over the hillsides with my staff raised high over my head, dragging those rain clouds. When I returned I had used up everything I had. I almost died dragging those thunderclouds, but I knew I had to make it back or others would die."

"When you came back, you were drained. You seemed so small and changed after that, and you finally looked at me..."

"It took all my strength and power to accomplish the task of bringing rain to our people. When I returned, I knew that I was at the end of my life."

"You laid down on that cot, remember?"

"In that hut..."

"Yes." I stopped and looked at him. Would he remember what he did after he died? Would he know he passed his staff on to me? I was suddenly aware of a ringing silence within me.

Trevor looked into my eyes. Were they as intense now? Did he know what I was thinking? So much was communicated without words between us in that lifetime. What about now? Did we still have the same abilities?

"You had the power within you all the time. I didn't give it to you."

He knew what I was thinking.

"But, man, those eyes! I could feel your contempt and I was uncomfortable when you would stare at me!"

Was he still afraid of me? I looked into his eyes and he held my stare. We smiled and then realized the others were silently waiting. We turned simultaneously outward to face the room.

"Then I became chief." I finished my story quietly, without Trevor's boisterous gestures and without his finishing my sentences.

"When Elaine told us to go to the time of our death, I just knew it was time and lay down on the same cot. The moon was full and..."

I stopped and looked off into the distance. "I remember this part vividly from dreams in my childhood. I remember looking out the window at the moon and very peacefully closing my eyes."

My emotions took control and I began to cry. "After I

left my body I looked back down and touched my daughter. She would be the next chief."

Elaine remained silent.

"It was so beautiful and peaceful."

Someone passed me some tissues and I attempted to wipe away an onslaught of tears.

Overwhelmed with thoughts and emotions, all I wanted to do was to be alone to consider the messages. A moment to talk with Trevor and see what he thought would really help. But other people began to comprehend what happened and they told me about Trevor and how hard he had tried to remain quiet and composed when I began my story. Everyone else in the room seemed to want to share their own opinions and versions of what they saw and heard.

"When you started telling your story, it was so funny..."

"Yeah, cause Trevor looked absolutely floored!"

"He was trying to keep his mouth shut but his arms were flapping all over the place!"

"He could hardly stand to sit still and listen, but you

could tell he was trying."

I couldn't tell who was saying what. Everyone else in the room was a blur to me now. I nodded politely in response to their comments and looked for a way out. I looked around the room for Trevor. He wasn't there. Silently he had left.

CHAPTER TEN

IT'S ALL A MATTER OF CHOICE

Dreamtime: *I feel myself leaving my body. Looking back down I see it on the sofa facing North Star Mountain. I am drifting up above the trees and above the Continental Divide. Then suddenly my soul is in the body of a majestic bull elk running up the mountain. My breathing and heart rate become the same as the rhythmic pulsing of the elks as he/I leap over rocks and dart around trees. I, the elk, run swiftly up the rocky terrain of the mountain.*

My vision focuses on what is ahead as he/I climb confidently upward. He was in a hurry, and we climbed steadily never stopping to rest. I sense others following. Two other elk are close behind, and farther behind, forcing them onward...mountain lion.

I sat up on the couch and gazed out the big picture windows at the starry night. The majestic mountains that surrounded our home welcomed me back. I had drifted off to what I had hoped would be a deep sleep, but the thin air at this high altitude was helping me to have visions, many visions, and little sleep.

This vision felt more powerful than any other I had experienced so far. I *was* the elk, I *was* the mountain lion.

I looked around the room. Everything looked the same; the moving boxes still unpacked and the empty bookshelves. The house was quiet, but the winds had picked up outside. I looked out the window and saw snow blowing off the peak of North Star Mountain.

I laid back down and closed my eyes. I wanted to remember every nuance of the vision. I felt its power and presence were still with me, still palpable. I knew it was an omen of things to come. I could not comprehend in that moment that this was telling me the answers to my questions: "who am I?" and "why have I come?"

The flyer at the grocery store had caught my eye those first few days after arriving at our new home. The past life regression was on Thursday night and the Reiki training began the next day and extended over the weekend.

The day after my past life with Trevor was revealed I returned to Mark and Tina's home, locals who were hosting Elaine's classes. Most of the people who were there for the Reiki training had participated in the past life regression session with Elaine. And Trevor was there.

Elaine was as amazed as the others by the connection Trevor and I had found in our past life. As we gathered in the living room she acknowledged this incredible coincidence.

How did our souls know? How did we find each other? Was it planned by Spirit, or did we have a hand in it? These questions and more were asked by each of us.

Elaine had met Trevor back East when he came to her clinic to learn the First Degree of Reiki. He wanted to learn Reiki II, the second degree so when Elaine decided to come to Breckenridge, Colorado to teach, Trevor decided to fly out and meet Elaine for the class.

As our Reiki training was about to begin that Friday,

Trevor and I saw each other but barely said "hello." I wondered why I felt so uneasy around him. I watched his confident nature as we gathered in the living room. He took his usual spot on the couch — where he had sat the night before — and spread his wide arms across the back of it. His presence felt bigger and wider than the couch. His apparent strength made me feel even smaller and less sure of myself.

Once again I sat cross-legged on the floor, attempting to take up as little space as possible.

Others in the room were exuberant about the story Trevor and I had shared.

"That was sooo incredible! I told my boyfriend about it last night after I got home. He just could not believe it!" began a woman with long brown hair and glasses.

"I know what you mean. My husband didn't believe it at first either. He thought maybe it was a hoax put on by the teacher," another student began to babble about my other life.

"Oh, Juli, you should have seen Trevor carrying on after you left last night. He kept talking about what you looked like and about your eyes."

116

That got my attention. *What all did he say? Where was he? He must have still been here when I left, but I didn't see him.*

Trevor sat silent and strong behind me.

"Okay, let's get quiet. Everyone find a comfortable place so we can begin." Elaine's quiet voice and Boston accent drew us in.

"I have some medicine cards that I will pass around. Each of you should draw a card and then I'll pass around the book that tells about each card. These medicine cards can help you get in touch with your own animal spirit, or totem. Each card has a different animal. The card you pick is the animal spirit or energy that is working with you at this time. So let's go ahead and pass the cards around. The book will come around after."

I had the same deck at home, along with several Tarot decks that I used regularly. Closing my eyes, I held the deck reverently before pulling a card. I passed the deck on as I stared at the figure on the card. Frightened by the animal that seemed to be leaping off the card at me I quickly placed it face down on the carpet in front of me.

That dream I had just the other night, what was that?

Suddenly the images came back and while the others contemplated their cards, I felt myself drift off into a trance-like state...

Once again I am in the body of a healthy, full-grown male elk. I am running up a mountain, strong and steady. I climb the mountain with confidence. I hear the snorting sounds of others behind me. My attention turns to the one behind me and now I find myself in the body of another elk, female this time. She is close behind the stag before her. My hooves carefully land over rocks and I duck branches of trees as we dart here and there, following the quickest path to...

I hear more breathing behind me and I am in the body of yet another elk cow. She is following the two in front of her. There is a sense of urgency along with assuredness. The pace quickens as I hear a hissing breath behind and the spine tingling cry of...

I am now in the body of the hunter — mountain lion. This is the being that has caused the chase. I see the hooves of the elk before me as she dashes up the mountain. With fire in my veins I follow my passion...

"Juli, what animal spirit picked you?"

MYSTIC MOMMY

Elaine's voice was always bringing me back, it seemed. Startled, I returned to the room.

I turned the card over and stared at it as I spoke ever so softly: "mountain lion." Silently the book was passed to me. I fumbled for a moment looking for the correct page.

I wish I weren't so nervous sharing these things in front of everyone. I'm just reading a page in a book. For heaven's sake, get a grip, Jules.

"Mountain Lion...O kingly leader, of sleek, feline form, touch my heart with courage, then sound the alarm, that I may lead with foresight, assurance, bright and true,..." I cleared my throat and nonchalantly wiped my weepy eyes with the back of my sleeve,

"To carry on the spirit of the strength I see in you."

I had finished the opening poem and had two more pages to read about mountain lion as my totem. My spirit was in my heart and my heart was in my throat. My eyes and nose were running. I couldn't believe that this message was appearing to me here today. I paused hoping for someone to save me, but the room was silent.

"Mountain Lion — Leadership." I cleared my throat

again and again but little came out.

This was a cruel joke Spirit was playing on me. How could someone who doesn't even have the courage to read two pages out loud have any leadership qualities? I guess I knew what it was saying to me, I'd always known what was deep inside me. The potential was enormous. But not now. Not here.

"Mountain Lion can be a very difficult power totem for you to have, because it places you in a position ..." the truth had caused me to lose my sight. The tears were backing up because I was frozen and afraid to blink. Was this for real?

"Matt, will you read it for me?" I whispered to the man next to me.

As Matt read I started trembling, just like I had the night before. The truth was hard to accept right now and I felt embarrassed by the words being read. Me?! A Leader?! **Everyone** in the room must be laughing inside.

Matt was reading loudly and clearly but only I heard the words Spirit whispered between the lines.

"If mountain lion has come to you in dreams, it is time to stand on your convictions and lead yourself where your heart takes you..."

Okay, no one else knows about my dream...I'll just keep that to myself. And where does my heart want to go? What are my convictions?

"...if you are aligned with cat medicine, you are considered to be 'King of the Mountain,' and never allowed to be human or vulnerable. The pitfalls are many..."

Am I trying to be superhuman? Do I have a tendency to expect myself to be perfect?

"...Therefore the first responsibility of leadership is to tell the truth..."

I'm not doing so well with any of this...I can't even face my own personal truth.

As usual Elaine was reading my mind. She gave me a penetrating stare and spared me her usual introspection. As she moved on to the next person I had time to take a few deep breaths.

I felt so embarrassed and vulnerable, as if everyone had just found out more secrets lurking within me.

Matt and Trevor and Rita shared their animal spirits and reflected on what was happening in their lives. Everyone was amazed at how accurately the descriptions in the book matched the events unfolding in their lives and the attributes needed to get them through. I remained sullen, questioning Spirit's message to me — a mother, homemaker, wife. A leader? I didn't think so. Not now, anyway.

I silently reflected on the mountain lion spirit that had appeared in my dreams for the past year. In the beginning she was hiding in a cave, watching me. Then, just as we moved to Colorado she wasn't in the cave anymore, and not knowing where she would turn up was even more frightening. Now when I went to sleep at night she was there, watching and waiting. And in the vision from the other night she had leaped into action. Was I supposed to follow her lead? She was chasing three full-grown healthy elk up a mountain. What did that mean?

The rest of the weekend was about Reiki. We received our attunements and as a group remained respectful and quiet throughout the process. Trevor and I avoided each other. At first I didn't know why, but on the last day the deep place Reiki brought me to showed me my true feelings. I noticed how we competed with our stories, with our healings, with our lives.

Why? Did I want to prove something to him? Was I jealous of his abilities and the attention Elaine gave him?

Jealous? Of Trevor? I didn't want to admit it, but I knew it was true. But why would I have those feelings in this lifetime?

I reflected during break as I sipped some herbal tea. Trevor and I had been competing the entire weekend. He was one step ahead of me in the Reiki training and I couldn't stand it.

Why was I jealous of him and his abilities now? Was it a carry-over emotion from another life and time?

The questions poured through my mind: *What am I doing with my life this time? How do I spend my time? Where is my passion? Can I be that woman in Africa? Do I have the same abilities? Is there any leader inside me?*

My children were my life. I loved my husband. He was my partner and my best friend. I loved my children dearly. I would do anything for my family. Yet there was such an emptiness and so many insecurities that kept me bound to them out of fear. What was I afraid of? Why did I feel like I was hiding who I really am behind my family? Was I just the mountain lion waiting and watching from the cave?

And my dreams! What about all those dreams? Callings I have had to heal others. I remembered what the angel had said to me a year ago: "Just touch people." Was I doing that? No. I was too busy doing dishes and folding laundry.

How I wished I could do more, but I loved my children so very much. For some reason I equated love with being there, being there for them as much as possible. I couldn't yet see that my own growth and fulfillment would be another way of loving them.

I felt guilty for even having thoughts of wanting more than what I already had. Yet I did make it to these classes, even though it was a bold step for me and a sacrifice for my family. They weren't used to my being gone at all, let alone for three, whole days. *Why did I feel so guilty about leaving them?*

As I looked around the room I felt as if my head were in a cloud. I wondered if my life was any different this time around. Was I hiding my talents and my power? Did I use my family to keep myself hidden?

Elaine stared at me. She knew. It made me uncomfortable when she picked up on my thoughts. I suppose what really made me uncomfortable was that I picked up her answers.

"Perhaps you need to walk around outside and ground all the energy coming into you. We are receiving a great deal today with these attunements."

I smiled shyly and stepped outside.

Standing on the front porch I breathed in the thin, intoxicating, mountain air. Looking around I was in awe of the fabulous snow-covered peaks. There was a crisp, Fall chill in the air and my wool sweater was just enough to keep me from being too cold. I peered down the driveway and felt the forest beckoning me to connect. Slowly I strolled past Elaine's temporary trailer home in order to walk down the empty, dirt road.

Before reaching the road I stopped abruptly when Trevor appeared from the other side of the trailer.

"Oh...hi. I didn't know you were out here." I said feeling awkward and embarrassed fearing that he might think I had come looking for him. He had remained reclusive this final day of training.

"I went for a walk." He was silent as he looked past me. "I guess I'll go in now."

He hesitated and I really wanted to say something! I

wished we could clear up whatever walls we had built so long ago. Why were we brought together? Why did Spirit have us see our past life together? Certainly there was some work left do, but Trevor would fly back to Boston tomorrow and I might never see him again!

"So...what do you think about the Africa thing?" *Thing!?! Did I really say that?* I wanted to hide...*thing! He must think I'm so immature!*

"I don't know...I have a lot to think about. I'm not sure what I'm supposed to do....Elaine kept talking about it last night." He spoke but his words didn't feel directed toward me.

"Yes, I feel like everyone else is so excited about it." I was puzzled by my lack of awe about what happened. The fact that Trevor is here made me want to understand something more, but all I could see was my inability to stand-up for myself, both then and now. I kept waiting then for someone else to "bless" me, just like I was waiting in this lifetime.

"You really need to forgive me."

His sudden candor grabbed my attention. I quit staring at the ground and looked into his face. He was speaking to me this time.

"You realize, I hope, that you chose to not use your powers. Everything that happened, you chose it to be that way. It was your experience and it wasn't my fault. Everything you do is your choice. You chose to put yourself in that position then and I guess maybe you are now, too. You can't keep blaming other people, you know. If you choose not to use your gifts, that's your choice. But don't go blaming others. Decide what you want to do...and do it." Trevor looked into the mountains. His voice was quiet again and he was no longer speaking to me, "That's what I need to do...decide..." His voice trailed off and once again he was absorbed in his own life and its meaning.

I was stunned. I needed to forgive **him**? I wasn't so sure. I wasn't mad at him. I was mad at myself.

Well, maybe I was waiting for someone to give me permission to use my gifts. Maybe I was waiting for someone to tell me what my gifts were and what to do with them.

Maybe I needed to go home and take care of my responsibilities. Maybe I needed to be a better mother and quit taking these silly classes.

Then again, maybe Trevor was right. Maybe I needed to quit looking outside myself for validation and maybe I needed to quit blaming everyone else. I needed to look at my circumstances. I needed to grow. I knew this but I wasn't ready to let go of the easy path of playing the victim.

I felt flushed and noticed I had grown sweaty in the cool air. I hurried back inside and barely spoke the rest of the day.

That evening we all said our good-byes. Some of the other locals who had taken the Reiki Class agreed to have me over for a Reiki Circle the following week so we could practice giving Reiki and to support each other as healers.

Elaine took down my address and phone number. We talked about the next step, a Reiki II class which she suggested I take the next time she came to town. I wanted to take the level II class that Trevor had just finished.

Of course I'd have to ask my husband about taking more classes. I wasn't sure that I should spend the money and the time on more healing classes. Couldn't the others see I didn't have a choice? My family had to come first. Was I mad at my husband for that? Was I still mad at Trevor?

I turned around after giving Elaine and the others warm

hugs good-bye. Trevor was standing there waiting his turn.

We looked into each other's eyes without sentiment and said, "good-bye."

CHAPTER ELEVEN

LOUISA

Dreamtime: *I am traveling on a train that is moving at high speed through mountain passes. As I approach an open doorway I don't hesitate for a moment, I simply step off of the moving locomotive. Still upright, I walk away.*

I am wearing a transparent dress, a lovely, floaty, gauzy thing and it reveals everything. I am baring all and I don't seem to care.

I closed my eyes and held the deck of tarot cards close to my heart. I felt hesitant to lay them out on the table in front of the other women. After a deep breath I began to turn them over in the way our teacher had instructed.

"This spread of the tarot shows the life path of the individual. It is based on the ancient Kabalah, which is the tree of life. It shows the person's connection to the Divine and the path they have chosen on Earth to reach that state. Here at the bottom we see the basic challenges faced on the physical level, then the emotional challenges and so on to the top level."

I curled my shoulders and shuffled the rest of the deck nervously in my lap. The cards on the coffee table revealed all my insecurities as well as my habits. I merely glanced at them and felt as if I had bared all to the others in the Advanced Tarot Class. I knew each one of them could read the cards as well as I and I feared what they would find out about me.

The other three studied the cards quietly for a moment. Then the most outspoken of the group, a dynamic woman with red hair and a small, wiry frame burst out as she stared incredulously at me, "YOU don't like yourself?!"

The others nodded in agreement as they dissected the layout of the ten cards I had placed before them.

MYSTIC MOMMY

"You *really* don't like yourself! I mean...REALLY!" a shy woman, also named Julie, studied my face as she spoke.

They all knew it must be true, the cards never lie and each one of the women gathered to study together were seeing the same thing in the cards laid out on the table.

They stared at me in amazement for a moment. I guess I seemed self-confident. I carried myself with a high head and a smile. I seemed to have it all. There was the lovely home, the adorable children and a kind husband. How could this be?

I hugged my knees to my chest and blinked back the tears. The women sensed that a deep-seated truth had just been brought out into the open and turned to the cards to look for some uplifting revelations about me. But there was more to be said that kept me quiet and somber.

"You have a very romantic nature and romanticize about every aspect of life. I think you are always disappointed when life falls short of how you imagine it could be." The teacher, Kaya, pointed out the card that illustrated this and the placement of it in the tree of life spread.

A slight nod to Kaya, was all I managed, but she understood completely. I felt a sense of completeness that baffled me. Someone was beginning to see who I really am, yet it was all making me feel so vulnerable.

Kaya reminded the class that everything revealed and seen in the course was to remain confidential among the four of us. They all understood as they looked for more to analyze.

"You have had a lot of changes in your life and it seems that you initiate them. Notice the transformation card at the base of your being. It seems as though as soon as you start something, it is done and you move on," Julie pointed to the Death Card at the base of the spread as she explained. Clearly major change was a part of my life path.

Another student countered, "I don't know that you even finish things in the physical world. You are very connected to Divine Energy and you are constantly inspired – to the point that you transform and move on before your ideas show up on the physical level. You learn and transcend more quickly than the physical world can mirror your change."

The teacher turned to me and queried softly, "Have there been a lot of big changes in your life during the last ten years or so?"

"Yes, you might say that! I've moved a couple dozen times and have had more jobs than that! I feel like I am constantly expanding and learning and my life feels restricted so quickly...like I have to move, to make major changes in order to grow spiritually...does that make any sense?"

Kaya gave me a deep compassionate smile and turned back to the spread on the table. "It looks to me that once you get mastery over your physical world your connection to the Divine will take you to great heights, so to speak! We can see that the energy and drive you have will bring you success, once you accept the physical world as less than what you have imagined it to be. This world will never be able to match the vision you have, the utopia you picture for yourself and others. Just know the more you can accept the inadequacies of others the more quickly they will rise to meet your great expectations and your own life will expand to meet you. Accept life as it is now and then your vision will flourish."

The others searched the cards for where Kaya was seeing this.

"Where do you see that?" asked Emily, who always doubted her ability to read, even though she was never mistaken.

"It's all over the place. Don't look so hard. Just let the information come through you." Kaya studied the faces of the class, "Let's do you next, Emily."

I gathered up my cards and wrapped my deck carefully back in the azure silk scarf to keep it generating positive energy. Then I laid it in my lap and looked without focus on Emily's spread. I shared very little the remainder of the time. When it was time to go, as I was putting my notebook and pen in my bag, Kaya asked if I would stay a little longer and do a reading for her.

"Me? Read for YOU?! I couldn't do that." Self-doubt gripped me.

My deep-seated, injured sense of self hadn't been news to me but what had left me feeling bitterly alone was that this defect, as I saw it, didn't appear in anyone else's spread. They had their own stuff to work on, but they were astounded by my true feelings about myself. And now I thought Kaya was trying to make me feel better by asking me to do a reading for her.

"I really need some help," Kaya said, "I'm working on some applications for a business venture and I'd like you to see what the cards are saying. You know how difficult it is to read the cards objectively for oneself."

Kaya was sincere so I pulled the carefully wrapped cards out of my sequined tapestry bag. I sat down on the couch and Kaya came and sat next to me. I laid out the cards and told Kaya, with great hesitation, what I saw and what I felt would happen.

Kaya nodded in agreement, "That's what I thought."

"Now," Kaya said, "let's lay out my Kabala Spread. I haven't looked at it in ten years, at least." She said it with great finality as if this were what she really wanted me to see.

I laid out the ten cards, studied them and looked at Kaya. This spread more closely resembled mine than any of the others I had seen that evening. Kaya had known what the cards would say and intuitively I knew this was why she had asked me to stay.

"So...what do you see?" Kaya asked very openly. She smiled and her body remained open to her truth.

I was afraid to speak the entire truth. I greatly admired Kaya, who had more psychic abilities than anyone else I'd ever known. She was well-read and had a great sense of humor. She had done so many things in her life already and she looked no older than her mid-thirties, although considering her experiences I'd have thought she must be much older. Perhaps she knew a magic spell to remain looking young.

"Start at the top." Kaya helped me out, "What are my feelings about God?"

"You don't know. You're confused sometimes and doubt a lot of the time."

"Yes." I was surprised to see her swallow hard. She helped me go down the spread and showed me the secrets of her own life. More insecurities showed up - in her physical world as well as the spiritual.

"I can't believe how this shows all of me!" Kaya motioned to the cards with her palms up. "I feel so exposed!" She laughed and crossed her arms to cover her chest.

"I know. That's how I felt." We stood and embraced warmly. Then I readied myself for the long drive home across the snow covered mountain pass.

"Good-night, Juli. See you next week," Kaya called from the open door as I crawled into my car.

"Okay! Bye." I closed the door and fumbled with the seat belt.

As I headed down the dark mountain roads my eyes began playing tricks on me. I slowed to thirty-five miles per hour in case any of the apparitions crossing the road were real.

Visions of elk, deer, coyotes and foxes dashed across the road in front of me. I trembled from the chill still inside the vehicle — or was it from seeing the ghostly appearances? I wasn't certain whether what I was seeing was an illusion so I kept braking, feeling certain that an apparition could knock me off the road.

"I thought I was better!" I cried out to the animal spirits that danced across the road. "I thought I liked myself! I've been working so hard at it. I've read a lot, meditated, had treatment and therapy and tonight, the first thing they saw was, 'YOU don't like yourself?!'"

I kept hearing the women's voices and seeing their shocked looks as they examined my cards. And now the Universe seemed to be laughing at me as well. I was seeing so many ghostly things. What was happening? Had the spirit world decided to let me see everything tonight? Had I passed a test, or was I going insane?

Tears started to well up in my eyes and I pulled over to the side of the road. I prayed for guidance. "Just get me home safely. Please."

After a moment my vision cleared — or was it blocked? Now unable to see the spirits around me, I placed trust in the unseen forces to help me get home safely. I was glad to be able to focus on the road. I trusted Spirit and my well-meaning animal guides to take me home.

An hour later I drove up our steep driveway, stepped out of the car and breathed a sigh of relief. I inhaled the clean, cold mountain air and looked around at the snow in the starlight. The mountains around me made me feel safe. I greeted the mountains and stars I knew by name and went inside the house.

It was dark and quiet inside and my husband was asleep in bed with the children, an open book lying on his chest. I kissed each girl quietly on the forehead and gently shook my husband, Ted, awake. He woke up enough to inquire about class, but not enough to hear my answer. He wandered into our bedroom and I went into the living room.

"Why?" I asked North Star Mountain. From the living room window, I looked to my guiding star. It winked at me and I lay down on the couch.

MYSTIC MOMMY

Safe at home, I let the tears fall.

These women had found out several of my deep, dark secrets and I trusted them with the information, but I would never forget the looks on their faces and the terrible embarrassment I felt when I had to admit to them how accurate the cards were.

When my tears became a trickle, I relaxed and focused on meditating. I connected with Spirit and asked, "Why is it? Why do I have such low self esteem?"

I had suffered from low self-esteem since I was a small child. Others seemed so surprised when they realized how deeply my insecurity ran. It felt like a knife that turned and twisted inside me whenever I tried to look at it.

I felt astounded that it was still as deep and gruesome as ever. I had been working hard at overcoming these feelings and the cards revealed that these insecurities were not just from a troubled event in my childhood. This wasn't a scar. The cards told me this was a much older wound. Something I was born with.

Again I asked Spirit, "When and how did these insecurities become an integral part of who I am?"

141

Immediately I felt my body spinning. With my eyes closed I lifted off like a rocket and I knew Spirit was carrying me through the ethers. I relaxed and allowed myself to be taken away. The answers to my questions were not far away. Just as quickly as I was spun out of my physical world I felt myself land in another time and space.

I looked down and saw petticoats — many layers — and a gray dress. My hands were hidden in gloves. She was hiding herself, I was hiding myself. I saw it immediately and I sensed this girl that I am, or was, was named Louisa.

There was a knowing within me that said I was in France. The home I was in was very regal. It felt like a palace, but my life was not elegant. I was shunned and kept hidden. I was deformed, although there didn't seem to be anything wrong with me physically. I felt ugly and misshapen, although it might have been my posture that made me feel this way. I was hunched over and uncomfortable in my body.

My garments felt heavy on me. Besides the petticoats, heavy skirts and gloves I, also wore a bonnet. These garments were intended to hide me. They were not fancy clothes, but plain and of simple fabrics. My face felt ugly. I wanted to remain hidden.

MYSTIC MOMMY

The year was 1642 and I was an illegitimate child to the King of France.

These facts came to me as I stood in Louisa's shoes, which were buttoned up the ankle and back. Louisa spent a great deal of time looking at them, for she rarely looked up.

"You're not good enough." I, as Louisa, heard this over and over.

The home I lived in was rich and opulent but I was ugly and not something that royalty wanted to see. I was a deformed being, an outcast. I was an embarrassment to my mother and not considered alive by my father.

I rarely saw my mother. A dark-haired man, short and heavy-set, came to see me. He told me, "You're not good enough."

My mother did not want anyone to know I was her daughter, not because I was a bastard child, but because of how I looked.

I thought I was somewhere outside Paris, Versailles perhaps. I was in a room with red, velvet curtains surrounding large windows that reached up to the ceiling. Looking out the window I saw other children playing outside.

Suddenly I remembered that this room was meant to be off limits to me and I hurried back upstairs to my playroom. It felt very cold and gray. It was big and filled with toys, but I was always alone, I had no playmates. Most of my time was spent weeping and staring out of the windows.

The other children saw me from time to time and ridiculed me and my deformed body. They laughed merrily as they teased.

When I was eight or nine I traveled to the country. I was sent to live with a kind woman in southern France. She was very kind to me, as were other people in her village. She took me with her to market and all about the town. For the first time in my life I felt accepted and was able to go where I pleased.

Occasionally I was sent back to Paris. I wanted to see the city, but was only allowed to go out at night, when no one would see me. It seemed that my mother sent for me to come to Paris. I was never sure why.

I felt the vision leaving. Something was pulling me back to my present form.

I didn't want to leave Louisa. I loved her and I tried to tell her so over and over again.

MYSTIC MOMMY

She faded away as I spun farther and farther away from her, yet I called again and again, "I love you, Louisa."

I sensed my body again. I felt the couch beneath me, but still I tried to reach back for her. After experiencing other past lives I had been able to access the other forms I have been. I wanted to talk with Louisa, but she was reluctant. Something was keeping us from connecting and I could not speak with her.

Again I told her I loved her and I reached out to hug her. She disappeared up and into the light coming from above me.

A spirit voice said, "That's all you need to know for now."

My experience with Louisa ended abruptly.

Sitting up I realized that my feelings then were how I felt about myself in this lifetime. No wonder others who got close enough to look within my heart came away shocked and confused, for inside I felt like an outcast.

Even as a child, I thought I was a misfit. Something didn't feel right inside me. I felt so different. Even though I had friends and was well-liked at school, I felt as though I was not in the right place. I didn't feel the same and that was a very unattractive feeling in itself.

Seeing this brief glimpse of Louisa's life hadn't given me an opportunity to heal. I wanted to reach her, to love her and help her heal so that I could also.

Spirit answered my question, "Why?" Now I wanted to know how to heal and I wondered if I would see Louisa again.

CHAPTER TWELVE

STARS IN MY HANDS

D reamtime: *I am in a big home – a mansion. This place feels unfamiliar to me. My daughter, Lauren, is upstairs getting dressed. This home feels almost like a grand old hotel and I am not totally comfortable h*ere.

Lauren comes downstairs. We descend to the lower level. It is a huge room filled with water. We are indoors, but this room opens to waters beyond. There is a sweeping view of a vast ocean beyond the large open doors.

A baby orca swims past. Lauren and I are joyously enthralled by this experience. Watching it so closely, we

147

don't see anything else. As it heads out to open sea I step back and realize the huge, sweeping white and blackness in my vision is the orca mother. She is passing so close and is so huge I cannot take in her entire being at one time. I see an eye looking deeply into me. Then her side passes by and little by little her entire vastness passes before me.

She is scrutinizing me and my child just as we are enraptured by her and her child. My breath is gone and my mouth hangs wide open...so real, I want to reach out and touch her. As I awake, she is gone.

A year after we had left our family and friends to move to Colorado, we were on the road again. I'd always felt a gypsy spirit within myself and my husband was happy to live a nomadic life as well, so off we went to live in the beautiful Pacific Northwest.

All we had to do was agree that it was where we needed to be, remain focused and soon we were driving into town with our children, dogs and luggage loaded in the Volkswagon pop-top van.

My guides had wanted us to go there all along. They seemed to help us along. Ted found a teaching position quickly and I enjoyed the many metaphysical classes.

MYSTIC MOMMY

We hadn't been in Seattle long and I was longing to learn more. As soon as Ted got home from school, I headed off to class.

I boarded the ferry and looked back toward my husband as he pushed Lauren and Grace in our jogging stroller. I felt as if I would not be seeing him again for a long, long time. In my mind it was a melodramatic goodbye out of a romantic novel.

As I stood on the deck of the ferry, the ferryman signaled my departure with the slow, low horn. My husband never looked back to see my teary face and my hand waving timidly, "Good-bye."

I remained on the deck, allowing the wind to dry my face. The water sloshed against the boat. The seagulls cried out in search of food.

"My hands are empty," I explained opening my palms, "I have nothing to give you today."

On the other side of the sound I walked briskly off the boat and up the street toward the shop where the palm reading class would take place. I stopped in the deli next door for a cup of herbal tea. The Fall air was chilly and I couldn't stop shivering.

A woman with jet black hair, dressed sharply in a black velour pantsuit, stood outside the deli talking with a man sitting on a bench.

I knew her. I knew this woman with the jet black hair. I couldn't remember where I had seen her before, but I knew her.

After finishing my tea I walked next door to the shop where the class was to take place and stopped momentarily in the doorway. What would happen here tonight? A dramatic feeling washed over me — something colossal was going to happen. First the farewell scene on the ferry where I felt as if I wouldn't be seeing my family for an entire lifetime, and now I felt an overwhelming, emotional foreshadowing.

I had just wanted to learn a little more about palm-reading. It had sounded like fun. Now it was feeling like another one of my out-of-body-out-of-my-mind-totally-spinning-out-of-control-out-of-this-world kind of night.

Suddenly my palms were sweaty and my stomach jumpy. I walked past the woman with the jet black hair who must have entered the shop ahead of me. As I looked for a seat I felt her eyes follow me. Goosebumps ran up and down my body. How did I know her?

I picked a seat a safe distance from the front. In front of me two women were talking. I took off my jacket and tried unsuccessfully to get comfortable. The woman with the jet black hair walked to the front of the group and introduced herself. Linda Limona, Master Palmist. I sat straight up in my chair.

As Linda shared her personal story of reading palms, I saw two things at once. One was the class as it was unfolding and the second was a scene from another time and place. I saw Linda transform into another being — a beautiful woman with golden hair and a scarf around her head. She danced around a fire that was built here, in a clearing in the woods.

I blinked my eyes and looked around the room, folding chairs, women in front of me and Linda at the front of the room. Here I was in a metaphysical shop in Edmonds, Washington. There were angels and incense for sale and a dozen or more people sitting quietly listening to Linda, the instructor for this evening's class. As she showed us the basics of reading palms, I tried to follow along.

The uneven thunking of wagon wheels knocking against uneven cobblestones, along with the clanging of pots and pans as they swung on their hooks on the gypsy wagon, made it difficult to ascertain which line on the palm Linda was explaining. The scenes kept shifting and I watched myself step into another life while I sat, eyes open, watching and listening to the informative talk about the ancient art of palm reading.

In the gypsy scene I saw another woman with dark hair and I knew she was my mother. Instantly I was aware that Linda was my mother's sister. I felt the recognition sweep over me like a tidal wave. I knew this woman teaching palmistry was once my aunt and I felt a deep love for her.

As the lecture continued I relived scenes from my gypsy lifetime. There seemed to be discontent between my mother and her sister and I often found myself caught in the middle. My mother, dark-skinned, dark-eyed, taught me the ways of the gypsies. I grew up knowing a nomadic existence. I felt the cold stares of townspeople as I walked alongside our caravan through town, pots swaying and clanking as we rolled along, my feet walking on cold stone roads. Head up, eyes straight ahead, I did not allow the judgments of others to stop me in my path.

Inside our gypsy wagon was a small wooden table where I worked with cards. I studied them, lived and breathed them and came to know everything about telling fortunes. I learned how to please men very early in life. I was participating in these scenes of my gypsy family playing music, drinking and laughing around a fire. Even as I sat in class I was also walking past everyone, leading a stranger to sexual fulfillment inside our wagon. I knew the smell of men and the lusty way they saw me. I felt contempt for them, laying their money on my bed. It seemed like a waste of their money and an easy way for me to live, for I knew nothing of sin, marriage, or shame. I only felt disgusted by what they did, not what I did. I was making money. I was in control of my life. I liked my body and I didn't need anyone.

Handouts in the classroom came to me and I took one and passed the rest. As I studied the sheet in front of me I recognized the drawings. Pictures of palms with all the lines labeled and brief descriptions of each glared at me, reminding me of the other time.

As the scene from the past continued to unfold, my body started to shake. I wondered whether anyone else noticed.

As I recognized Linda as my aunt in this other life, I remembered the loving tenderness with which she helped to raise me. I wanted to run to the front of the room and say, "Remember me?" I pictured her enveloping me in a warm embrace. Instead I listened intently.

I had seen my gypsy-self in dreams before. I

remembered my long, black hair and cappuccino-colored skin with eyes unlike my mother's. Mine were azure blue, clear and deep as pools of water. They looked mysteriously odd next to my dark skin and hair. I wore a white peasant skirt and lots of bracelets. I loved the sound of the metal on my arms. My white skirt and blouse felt cool and clean next to my dark, dirty skin. Through my bare feet I could feel the earth's energy and I pulled that energy into me.

But I was an outcast among outcasts. My mother preferred the company of men to her motherly duties. She ignored me when there was a man to be had. She loved the attention of men and regretted having a child about.

My aunt took me into her home sometimes. I lived with her and her lover, who stayed for while and then went away for days at a time. He had golden brown hair and blue eyes.

When I saw my aunt's lover with my mother, I recognized him as my father. The two women shared the same lover. That explained the animosity between them. My mother tried to keep him for her own, but he always returned to the home of her sister.

When Linda asked for volunteers to come to the front, my hand went up but I was not chosen until everyone else had had a turn. Linda looked at me as I stepped forward and took my quaking hand in hers. She studied my palm carefully, then looked into my eyes.

"Hmmmmm," was all she said for a very long time.

I sensed that she was stalling. The master palmist knew what was in my palm, but she refrained from speaking. She had not hesitated with anyone else's reading. I realized that my whole body was shaking and I was sure the others could see my hand shaking.

Does she think I'm nervous? Or does she sense my body remembering who we were?

I could barely stand to be so close to this woman who had taken me in and loved me as her own child once upon a time. I wanted to hug her. And I wanted to know if she recognized me.

Linda said, "Well, these lines here show how many children you have. You have two, right?"

I nodded. She looked for other things to mention, but I knew she was not sharing what stood out the most. After a long, painful silence, she turned me toward her, took both of my hands in her own and said, "Why don't we talk after class?"

The class tittered as I shyly took my seat.

As the class finished, so did my experiences in the other life. As a mature woman I came to live with my aunt. She had a home, a permanent home. I lived there alone in my old age after my mother, my aunt, and everyone else was gone. I continued doing readings and healings later in my life. Once I came to live there I ceased seeing men. And I was happy.

I lived peacefully and died peacefully.

I waited for everyone else to finish talking to Linda after class before approaching her. Many people from class wanted to schedule private appointments. I listened to women exclaim at Linda's accuracy in reading their palms. Everyone wanted more information. Linda's calendar was filling up. After the last appointment was set, I walked nervously toward her, wondering if she sensed any of the same things I had seen.

What should I say?

Not knowing what to say, I remained silent.

Linda opened her arms and took me in. She hugged me warmly for a moment. Then she held my hands as she looked into my eyes.

"It's going to be okay. I know you're going to do great."
Linda said sincerely.

I blinked back tears and didn't know what to say. "Do
you remember me?" I wanted to ask, but I felt that she was
seeing the here and now, not remembering what I had seen.

"You have these stars in your hands, see?" Linda pointed
to the "stars" at the end of my fate line, line of fame and
head line. I wondered why I had never really noticed them
before.

"They indicate great success!" She squeezed my hands
and looked at my palms again.

"You are going to do great. I see you standing at a
podium. I see people there, many people. They have come
to see YOU!"

Linda looked off above me as if she were seeing another
time and place.

"Yes. They are definitely there to see you." She paused
and looked at my hand again, "Do you write?"

"Yes. Well...I mean I journal. And I record my dreams and things..."

"Well, I think you need to do some serious research work and get busy writing!"

I thought about the kinds of research I was doing...past lives popping out all the time...

"You are also very psychic, aren't you?"

I looked down at my feet. I didn't want Linda to know how overactive my imagination was. If our eyes met she would know about my silly, past-life imaginings I'd had that very evening. How embarrassing that I thought we were gypsies together...

"Yes, you are very psychic. But you talk yourself out of every experience! You have a logic that wants to explain everything away. As soon as you have a psychic impression you go in a complete circle until you convince yourself you never had one."

She laughed, stepped back and looked me over from head to toe.

"You need to get those kids in daycare and get to

work...doing your research." Linda beamed a gorgeous smile at me.

I understood what she meant by research. But put the kids in daycare? I couldn't do that.

"Quit hiding behind your children. You are going to do great! Don't worry!"

I was still tongue-tied. There were so many things I wanted to ask Linda, but I lacked the confidence to speak up. I was trying to convince myself the psychic impressions of another lifetime with her were just another illusion.

Linda was right about my logical brain wanting to undo my experiences. I certainly could convince myself that my psychic impressions were nothing more than my imagination.

Could Linda be right about the other things she saw in my hands?

As I turned to leave, tightly clutching Linda's business card, she called to me, "If you ever want to talk, you know, woman to woman or...psychic to psychic...please, do call me."

I felt pleased. Maybe I would call her someday. After I convinced myself I really was psychic.

As I stood on the ferry anticipating its arrival at the dock, I realized I had been away a long time. I understood why I felt so melancholy saying goodbye to my husband earlier in the evening, for it had been a "lifetime" since I saw him. I was coming home knowing myself a bit better. And I was looking at life with renewed hope.

For I hoped what Linda said would someday come to pass...

With stars in my hands and clouds in my eyes, I went home. Home to hide behind my children a little longer and home to convince myself that this was all really happening to me.

CHAPTER THIRTEEN

THE PSYCHIC FAIR

A s more and more past lives were shown to me I felt myself becoming whole. I was gathering clues as to who I am and what gifts I have to share. Each lifetime revealed more truth about myself from the past and helped me to look at issues I had carried over into this lifetime. I was working quickly to get through my issues and fears.

The past lives were reminders of the potential that lives within me. I had come to realize the wisdom I had in the other lives was still within me, it doesn't go away. In my past lives I had the ability to read the cards, see the past and present at once, to see spirit guides and even to communicate with the dead...all these things I had done before. So why was I so surprised to find out I could do all those things now?

And what was I to do with these gifts?

What else could I do? I had to keep moving forward. I had to share my gifts with others. I saw in the other lifetimes how hesitation and doubt had led to frustration, depression and even death. Blaming others for my situation wasn't working. It only served to leave me more frustrated.

I didn't want to continue to blame motherhood and my responsibility to my children on my not sharing my gifts. I would only regret it later.

If I wanted to teach my children to follow their hearts, then I had to show them how by following mine. I wanted my daughters to learn to put themselves first. I knew I had to follow my own callings, even if it took me away from them on the weekends. That was all I could afford to give up in the beginning. Ted was home on the weekends, so I did what I could then.

I don't remember how I finally took that first step, it just happened because it had to. Telling people I was available for readings was perhaps one of the scariest things I had ever done. It happened despite my fears, insecurities and irrational doubts.

All I did was to share a few flyers and soon I was doing tarot readings for others. I was surprised when clients came back and shocked when they sent their friends and family. Then I found myself doing readings at psychic fairs, sharing my gifts with even more people.

I still remember my first psychic fair. I landed a spot at the last minute when another reader couldn't make it. The owners of the new age shop hosting the fair called me the day before to see if I was available to fill in. I was so thrilled and so scared.

Spirit carried me through that fair and each and every one thereafter. When I laid the cards out before me I opened up to the spirit world and information came.   Spirit was there for me, telling me what the people needed to hear.   And I did my best to listen.

"I don't know how you do it, but after being with you I feel so much lighter," a psychic fair client told me as she stood to leave, "like everything has been lifted off my shoulders."

I shrugged and gestured above. "I don't hang on to it. I

allow it to move on." I was happy to see her again. She had become one of my regulars and it was great to see familiar faces at the fairs. I was becoming comfortable in this atmosphere of healers and psychics.

As soon as her chair emptied, someone else hurried over to fill it. A well-dressed woman sat down across from me. The first thing I noticed was the huge diamond wedding ring on her wrinkled and aging hand.

She let me know that she was somebody special and that many of her friends would want to know about her reading. She made it very clear that she wanted a top-notch reading and she mentioned the column she wrote in the local paper.

So when I heard a voice in my left ear, a man's voice telling her she needed to let go of her marriage and to let her husband move on, I hesitated. This woman obviously loved her status. What would she think? Look at that diamond! It was probably over two carats! Tell her to leave her husband?

I imagined her laughing at me and leaving. I saw her telling her friends what a phony the tarot reader was. I could see the column in the newspaper calling me a charlatan...

The voice spoke to me again. "I didn't say she should leave her husband. Just tell her she needs to let go of her husband."

I couldn't deny what I was hearing. I'm not sure if I trusted the voices, but I was beginning to feel a deep respect for the other side.

Softly, in case people at the other tables were eavesdropping, I spoke: "You need to let go of your husband."

She looked at me with no expression. I couldn't read her face, it had turned to stone.

Bravely I continued. "I'm getting a very clear message and it is telling me that you need to let go of your marriage and let go of your husband." I waited for her to do or say something.

She turned her face away and looked off in the distance.

"How can I?" she queried with a trembling voice, "I love him."

The voice was there, and now it had a name.

"Earl says you need to let go..."

Suddenly a light came on in my head, "Is Earl your husband?"

She nodded and continued to avoid eye contact with me.

"By any chance is he...deceased?"

Again she nodded.

I paused and took it all in.   I wanted to jump up and tell someone what was happening. But that might tip her off that talking to the dead was a new talent I had just found. This was a first for me, as far as I knew. Instead I decided to play it cool and help her through her crisis...

"He died twenty-five years ago. But he is still with me. I make him dinner every night. I put his food on his T.V. tray in front of his favorite chair..."

She removed a well pressed linen hankie from her pocketbook and wiped her eyes. "I know he's there." Now she turned her gaze on me, "I can feel him. "

I nodded my understanding and acceptance of this truth in her life. It gave her permission to go on.

"We talk all the time. But...well, now there's someone else. I met someone..." she turned her attention away again. She felt ashamed to tell me.

I looked past her and I saw Earl.

"He's here with you now."

She looked into my eyes again for reassurance.

"Yes, I can feel him." But she looked at me, not at Earl. I guess I was the only one who could see Earl.

"He says you need to let him go. He is ready to move on ...and he says you need to be with someone..."

Her face flushed. That had a certain connotation in her mind.

"I understand. I know he's right. It's so hard though."

The manager of the fair gave me the time's-up sign by pointing at her watch and gesturing to the others waiting their turn for a reading.

"Thank you." She stood to leave and took a twenty-dollar bill out of her purse and put it in my basket.

Whew! Earl followed her out the door. I could hardly believe what I had seen and heard. Talking with the deceased...man, oh man. I suppose it's what she expected of me.

I was scheduled to do a lecture about past lives the second day of the fair and as I sat doing my readings my nervousness was mounting. I was also suffering from a dreadful cold and felt the virus sinking deeper and deeper into my lungs as the readings progressed. The cold, damp Seattle winter had taken a toll on me, and my fear was making things worse. Or perhaps my fear was taking a toll on me and the Seattle weather was making it worse.

For some reason I could not understand why so many people wanted to come and hear me speak about my past lives and how to access their own. It was a mystery to me why so many people had signed up for my lecture.

I looked across the table at the couple who stared wide-eyed, waiting for me to impress them. One of my favorite clients had sent them to see me. She had told them I was a really great reader and so now they wanted me to prove that to them. The only message I was picking up for them was that they wanted to be entertained. So they sat waiting.

"What can I help you with?" I asked them as I laid the

cards down in a stack and sipped some water. I tried to study the couple for something that might be of benefit to them and they continued to look at me as if I were a circus act.

"Nothing really. Tracy told us to come see you. She said you're really good."

"Yes, well, usually people have a question or problem that they would like some insight on. People want to know what is really going on in their lives and how they might best work through their problems. Others want to know what their path or calling is, in other words what their purpose might be. Sometimes people are having troubles in their relationship and we sort things out." I picked up the cards and held them close to me. I wasn't ready to hand them over.

They looked at each other, and then the girl said, "Well, maybe you could tell us what we'll be doing a year from now...or sometime in the future."

This was not an issue. They just wanted to be impressed with the fortune teller and that's not what I do. But their friend had told them how good I was. I shuffled the cards and tried to focus on the couple.

As I began to lay the cards before me, a tickle surfaced in my throat. I tried clearing it, but it grew and grew. I tried sipping water and it grew. I started coughing and when I tried to speak, only raspy words came out.

They wanted me to pull a rabbit out of a hat. I can't do this. I wondered how I could get out of doing this reading.

Cold sweat began to form on my brow. I felt dizzy and weak. I attributed it to a full day of back-to-back readings.

My eyes began to tear as I focused on the vision in the cards. I knew what was happening. I gathered the cards together and wrapped them back in my blue silk.

"I'm sorry. I can't do this."

The couple sat there staring, first at me and then at each other. They remained quiet and stunned, as if the tent had been brought down around them and the circus had just been cancelled.

"I can't..." was all that came out. My voice was gone.

I went into the bathroom and coughed painfully for several minutes. When it finally ceased I went to gather my belongings and to take my table down.

Cindy, the manager and owner of the store hosting the fair saw me coming.

"Can I get you some tea? There's a woman waiting for a reading from you. Could you do one more? Please?"

"Okay. One more," I squeaked out in a painful whisper. I set my things back up quickly and gestured for the woman to come over.

As she sat down across from me I could tell she'd been drinking heavily. Her bloodshot eyes looked pleadingly at me.

Immediately I was filled with information about her circumstances. They were extreme — extremely bad. And she wanted me to save her. She was looking for some piece of information that would tell her everything would be okay. She wasn't ready to change, but she wanted to know change was coming.

"I'm going to go gambling tonight," her thick tongue slurred the words rolling out, "Got any tips?"

"I can't. I'm sorry." I looked into her eyes, "My voice is going and this really hurts." At least I was being honest.

The owner came over after I let another customer leave so abruptly. Usually I went over my allotted time.

"Are you okay?" she asked with sincerity.

"I'm going home. I'll get a good night's rest." I swallowed hard looking for the power to finish the sentence, "And I'm sure I'll be better by tomorrow."

"Oh, I'm sure you'll be great by tomorrow. Remember, it's standing room only! We are so excited!"

As I packed my belongings I felt the knowing looks from all of the other intuitives in the room. With a flushed face I gathered my cards, table scarf and assorted power tools that had decorated my table. I went quickly to my car not wanting to speak to anyone else.

The country road home was long and dark.

"Why, God? All these people were counting on me tomorrow. Am I that afraid to speak?" I considered my prayers during the past week. What had I been praying for? "Let everyone coming to my workshop have the best possible experience." That's all I had wanted — that everyone who came would have a good experience. I wasn't concerned about my experience. And now it looked like I was going to let them down.

I sat quietly waiting for Spirit to give me an answer. Then I remembered that Nick Bunick was speaking at the Conference Center in Seattle the next day. How I wished I could go see him, but I had promised to do the lecture on past lives.

Nick was a man who had a past life regression and found out that he had been the apostle Paul. When I had read about him in the newspaper, I got goose bumps all over. Then a spine-tingling energy entered through the crown of my head, swept through my entire body and left through the bottoms of my feet. And I began to see visions of Christ's time — detailed visions.

I knew there was truth in Nick's message and the sensations in my body confirmed it. I really wanted to meet him. But I had already agreed to work at the psychic fair and I had been asked to speak on past lives the second day of the fair, the same time Nick would be speaking about his. It felt oddly connected.

As I drove home pondering my lecture the next day a voice spoke clearly to me, "Go see Nick."

"Okay." I agreed, "I'll go, but only if my voice is gone."

CHAPTER FOURTEEN

CR⬯☙⬯

WE ARE ALL THE MESSENGERS

The next morning I couldn't utter a syllable. I wrote my husband a note on a page of my journal: "Call Cindy. Tell her I've lost my voice and can't do the workshop. Tell her I am really, really sorry. And tell her I'll call when I can..." I passed the paper to Ted, and he looked at me with sympathy.

Then I jumped out of bed, showered and headed for the ferry. My good-byes were brief that day. I knew where I needed to go and what I needed to do. There was no hesitation or doubt and no guilt about leaving the children.

Sitting in my car at the ferry terminal, I felt like a school girl playing hooky. I slouched down low in my seat. If someone who knew me saw me there, waiting for the ferry, they might wonder why I wasn't at my lecture.

I arrived at the conference center a little late and ran up the escalators all the way to the sixth floor. As I approached the closed double doors I felt tingly and nervous.

After reading the article in the paper about Nick I began having visions where my mind flashed back to the time of Christ. I saw with incredible detail the persons around Jesus. I saw a home where everyone met and I felt with my own hands the table where they often sat and conversed. But I couldn't have been there. Not me.

I continued to have visions of that time — of being around Jesus. Then I read Nick's story in the book The Messengers, written by G. W. Hardin and Julia Ingram. I believed Nick's story, that he was Apostle Paul, but I just couldn't believe I was there, too. Yet...I knew if I could meet Nick and look into his eyes, I would know for myself whether or not I was there. And now Spirit had given me the opportunity to go and see him.

Why was this so hard for me to believe? I'd seen so many of my past lives — I'd been a shaman, a gypsy, a monk, part of a harem, the illegitimate daughter of a king, a witch burned at the stake, a prisoner, a servant, and an African tribal chief. If I could believe these other incredible roles I'd played, why was I doubting that maybe, just maybe, I had been alive at the time of Christ?

If I'd had any say in the matter, wouldn't I have requested that lifetime? Of course I would have been there, if I could have.

I glanced at my watch and thought, "Cindy must be announcing that my workshop is cancelled. I feel terrible letting so many people down, yet I feel like this is where I am meant to be."

I took a deep breath and opened one of the double doors just enough to slip into the room. I leaned against the doors, astounded by the multitudes of people in the room. Nick stood at a faraway podium and between us was a sea of people. I thought of the sixty-five who had expected to hear me speak in this same moment. I thought that was a good crowd for a past life workshop. But this — there were more than five hundred people here!

I found my way to an empty seat near the back of the room. Everyone else was listening attentively to Nick, but my head buzzed with the sounds of other peoples' thoughts, the after-effects of doing all those readings the day before, I thought. It always took a while to shut down the psychic connection.

Not wanting to hear others' thoughts I tried to focus on Nick's speech, but I couldn't. I felt someone's eyes staring at the back of my head.

I heard my mother's voice speaking to me as a child in church: "Don't ever turn around to look, no matter what — it's not polite." I remained face forward but fidgeted a little.

The eyes were penetrating. Someone was trying to get my attention. Perhaps it was someone I knew...maybe someone who knew I was supposed to be somewhere else today. I couldn't stand the suspense, I turned around.

A man standing at the back of the room was looking directly at me, but I didn't know why. I wondered why he was looking and why I had turned around. For a second we locked eyes. Just like when I met Trevor, I felt as though I knew him from somewhere.

Turning back around I studied the crowd more closely. *What's really going on here?* I asked myself and any guides who were listening, *Why are so many people here? Do they all want to hear Nick's message? Do they all believe his interpretation of what Jesus really said?*

Spirit listened to my query and the answers came flooding in through voices and feelings. Instantly I knew why they were here. Right in this room I felt dozens of Marys, a dozen Josephs, and even more Peters and Matthews .

My own feelings of confusion — along with a touch of hostility — begin to surface.

GOD! Why are you doing this? Making us believe we were there? And I believed, too! I was shocked and embarrassed that I thought maybe I was there.

And yet there was a place inside me that believed I was there. That I *knew* Jesus. I remembered our time together like it was yesterday.

I felt uncomfortable sitting there.

Suddenly I looked up and saw Nick welcoming G.W. Hardin to the stage and I realized that Hardin was the man I had felt looking at me moments earlier. Now he was on stage telling his story and accepting Nick's thanks for believing him. He was sharing the amazing coincidences in his life that had occurred since he'd met Nick.

Why had he been looking at me moments earlier? I listened uneasily to his speech then I had to leave. I couldn't sit still with my head buzzing. Everyone else's thoughts and feelings were annoying me. And anyway I felt like I already knew what Nick and G.W. were going to say.

I felt the message...I felt it being whispered into closed ears as it floated throughout the room: *Listen...Listen...who are you? Who are you? Everything and more. That is who you are. Remember...remember...remember why you came. Don't hide. Don't hide anymore...remember the truth of who you are and why you came...*

I felt so confused inside. All these coincidences - did I make them up? Thinking I was there...sheesh. Perhaps none of my other lifetimes were real either.

But then I remembered Trevor. That was real.

I rushed out of the double doors and down the hall to the ladies room. It was quiet there and my mind could be still without the distractions of other peoples' fantasies.

I looked into my eyes in the bathroom mirror. *Do I know you? Yes...yes...I do remember who I am and why I have come.*

I crackled my mantra into the mirror: "I know who I am and why I have come." I had been saying that everyday for so long,...hoping to know the truth of it one day. Today I had no voice, it was nonexistent. I thought it would come back now that I had discovered my charade. It was just my ego thinking I was there! I laughed at myself and fought back tears simultaneously.

I still felt a burning desire to investigate that lifetime further. But how? What could I do? I stepped out of the ladies room to see G. W. Hardin heading back into the convention hall just ahead of me.

I called to him, "Mr. Hardin," but my voice didn't cooperate. I picked up my pace to try to catch him before he reentered the conference chambers.

Just before he reached the door he stopped and turned around abruptly to face me. Did he hear me approaching him? Did he feel my presence as I had felt his?

Breathless and speechless, I attempted to explain why I was following him.

"I wanted to ask if I could have a chance to meet with Mr. Bunick. You see, I have to know the truth for myself and I felt if I could just speak with him for one minute, well, you see...I mean...can you schedule something? A consultation, or..." I am forcing a whisper.

He leaned in close to hear me. Then, shaking his head, he stood straight and spoke softly. "No. Nick can no longer see people. His schedule is too full."

Panic hit. An emotional tidal wave was coming toward me. I could feel the emotions about to take over.

"But you see, I'm supposed to be giving a lecture right now on past lives, but I lost my voice..."

He smiled with sweet understanding,

"And something told me to come here today instead."

"I know. I've heard so many incredible stories. Spirit, God, whatever you wish to call IT , is speaking to so many people. You wouldn't believe how many people I've met who feel they were there...that they were Mary. I'll have ten to twelve Mary's come up to me in each city!"

I felt so uncomfortable and agitated. I wasn't Mary. Why did he think I thought I was Mary? I was...

"And do you know what?"

He leaned in close again and talked almost as quietly as I had. His gentle, compassionate nature put me at ease. As he spoke I looked directly into his eyes.

"What?" I squeaked.

"I believe every one of them."

I kept looking at him. I didn't get it. How could there be so many Marys? Were we all fantasizing? Delusional? Did we want answers to help us cope with our insane world? I was wondering about my own sanity as he continued...

"I believe *everyone* who feels they were there and I don't think it matters who *was* there."

He leaned in even closer as if he were about to share a deep, deep secret. I listened with my whole heart. My voice was gone. I was an open channel. All I *could* do was listen.

"What matters is that the message gets out there. I don't care who was there...the message has to get through." He looks at me with more words that remain unspoken. I felt the rest of the message coming from beyond. In the silence I received the answers to my questions.

Suddenly things were clear. I understood that we were all there as one — as *the* one. Perhaps all this remembering was part of the collective unconscious. Perhaps it was all happening now and we could step into the other lives we referred to as "past" at anytime. Perhaps we saw what we needed to see at any given moment from other times. Perhaps we could all be Peter, Mary, Paul and even Jesus!

What I was reminded of was the call. Many are called, few are chosen. Many, many feel the calling, Nick's calling, Christ's calling and we have to share the message.

But who would? Who could? Few would find the courage and the power within to do it.

Few would rise above their insecurities and doubts and fears. But we had to get the message out...

"I don't care who as long as we get the message out." He looked me in the eye and I felt that these words were meant for me.

I smiled and thanked him. He felt like an old friend and I was reluctant to leave.

Smiling, I backed away slowly and then turned and bounded down the escalator and outside as quickly as I could.

MYSTIC MOMMY

Outside the rain had stopped and steam rose from the dampness as the sun beamed down on the Seattle sidewalks. I made my way back to the ferry, certain of my calling.

I would get the message out. I would share the message as it was channeled through my life, or lives. I'd share my stories. I needed to do this for myself and for my daughters. I had a message to share.

I remembered Trevor and smiled.

CHAPTER FIFTEEN

FINDING MY VOICE

The next day I awakened and immediately cleared my throat. I was overjoyed as I called out to my children. They bounded into my bed and hugged me tightly.

"Mommy! Mommy! You can talk!"

"Mommy, you found your voice!"

Yes, I did.

I laid back in bed and closed my eyes. What now? What was the message? I had felt it so clearly yesterday, but now the idea of sharing it was making everything so foggy.

Later that same day I visited Dolphin House to apologize in person for missing my workshop on past lives. Sheepishly I walked in. I felt as if I had committed a crime. How could I convince them that the day before I had no voice and now I was fully recovered?

I wanted to tell Cindy everything — I knew she'd understand. But she was so excited she couldn't wait to tell me what had happened.

"Juli, we couldn't get a hold of most of the people who were coming to hear your talk. Many of them were taking ferries and had already left home when we got word you couldn't make it. So here we were with a room full of people. We were about to go in and break the news when this woman walked in and said that Spirit had told her to come here at two o'clock."

"So here I was wondering what to do and she announced that Spirit had told her to come. Then she just stood there and looked at us! I had a feeling her appearance wasn't a coincidence, so I asked her if she knew anything about past lives. Guess what? Well, I'll tell you what — she smiled and whipped out this book from her bag and said, 'I wrote a book about mine!'

MYSTIC MOMMY

"So we ushered her into the room that was filled with
people waiting for your workshop. And she absolutely
wowed and amazed everyone! Isn't that incredible!"

"Oh, that is so fantastic!" I let out a huge sigh of relief.

Cindy continued to tell me about this incredible woman.
She had spent the last twenty or more years as a
professional healer and psychic. I felt myself being eased
off of my own pedestal. I was relieved and a touch envious.
Well, I thought, someday I would have twenty years'
experience and maybe even my own book about my past
lives...

They were so excited about their new psychic that I
refrained from sharing the rest of my story. I was grateful
that Spirit had answered my prayers. All I had asked for
was that everyone attending would have the best possible
experience. And they had.

And, thanks to Spirit, I had heard what I needed to hear.

I headed home knowing my life was shifting and that I no
longer had to hide. For the first time ever I felt confident —
confident about my calling and my talents and confident
about sharing the true me.

And there was a message growing inside me. A message I knew would eventually need to be expressed. A message too big to remain hidden.

The message was about the power within each of us. The power is in us to heal, to bring rain, to feed the hungry. We are all capable of doing so much more than we have ever dreamed possible!

There is a tremendous amount of knowledge and wisdom within every one of us. How can we suppress what we have to share? How can we allow our doubts and worries to hold us back?

We are the healer, the shaman, the messiah, the dreamer, the artist and even the mystic.

Be who you are. Remember why you have come...for it is time.

It is time.

☙❧❀❧☙

CHAPTER SIXTEEN

EPILOGUE

Six years later...I had just finished typing my book. For a moment I sat back and enjoyed the feeling of completion.

I DID IT! I congratulated myself warmly as I collapsed into bed.

I really *did it! At last! I wrote my book!* I have shared my story! Oh, thank you, thank you, Dear Ones!

Thank you, Spirit! Joyfully I closed my eyes and attempted to quiet my mind. I thought of all the false starts — all the times I wanted to write but allowed day-to-day life to get in the way. What was I really afraid of? How could I be so afraid of this kind of success. This feeling of real accomplishment, it felt so great!

All that fear that had gripped me, that kept me from sharing what I know seemed so silly now. Of course this was why I came — to tell my stories.

I used to worry about not focusing all my time and attention on my children. I was totally wrong about that, too. Since I began focusing on my book, they had unleashed their own incredible talents. Now they were more aware of who they are and why they have come.

I recalled all the times I wanted to be more than a mom and felt so guilty for wanting to be more. I am being a better mom, now, because I am better to myself. Because I'm now true to my callings, they are learning to be true to theirs.

What kind of example was I setting before? The message I was sending was to give up your dreams — to put others first and yourself last...

But now I could kick back. Finished! Hooray!

MYSTIC MOMMY

I let out a heavy sigh and closed my eyes. Taking four long slow breaths, I managed to find inner peace. For a moment I felt nothing but warmth, then I saw a golden light.

As I relaxed more deeply I saw a form emerging from within the golden sphere of light. It was me — the self I once was — as my own guide. It was the woman from Africa. It was me as the chief from Africa.

She looked so beautiful. Was she before? I never noticed. I had never noticed this glow about her.

Her hair was wrapped in a turban of bright colors and she wore a white gauze tunic. On her feet were leather sandals. She approached me from a foggy background.

"Thank you, thank you, dear woman. Thank you for your story."

Her eyes twinkled merrily. The deep and penetrating eyes that used to intimidate were now like endless pools of water. I now saw a peaceful strength within her.

"I am so happy. It is finished!" I exclaim.

Her lips were pursed and they turned up at the corners.

She smiled and nodded to me in agreement.

"I am happy I could be the one to give this message, especially to mothers everywhere," I tell her.

She continued to smile and nod. I wished she would share with me just a little bit more, but she stood there looking like the cat had got her tongue!

"I am finished, right? I feel like I could just relax and play with the kids now. It was fun, but I'm kind of glad it's over..."

Her body started to shake and her lips parted. She let out a beautifully lifting laugh. It grew and grew as her head tilted back and she held her stomach.

"What? Huh? What's so funny?" I seemed to be in the dark again.

She looked at me one last time and then with a smile she turned to leave.

Many figures waited for her on the horizon. They were other versions of me. I recognized myself. I knew some of the forms. There was the Native American shaman, the Egyptian high priestess, the gypsy, the deformed young

French girl, a monk and still others. I didn't know them all, but I knew they were all me.

The woman I was walked into the crowd and she and the others merged into one. Every entity that I have ever been became one; one giant ball of light. FLASH! The ball of light exploded and then disappeared.

They were gone.

What now?

I heard my children laughing in the next room as my awareness of the here and now returned.

That feeling of completion had vanished.

The longing to know more, to do more, to understand more had returned. I wanted to follow those images, those Dear Ones, back into the other world. There were more good stories over there, I just knew it.

Instead of feeling like I had just finished something great, I felt as though I had opened a door to a whole new world.

Maybe I wasn't finished yet. Perhaps there would be

more — more lifetimes, more healing, more me and of course, more stories.

Where's my cloud? Time to cross the bridge. I can't wait to meet me again in another place and time.

❀ ☾ ❀

About the Author

The original subtitle of this book was My Many Lives. Beyond the professional intuitive and spiritual teacher, beyond the metaphysician and healer, beyond the author and speaker, beyond the woman and mother, the titles describing Cat RunningElk span gender, geography, and generations. She is the Native Shaman, the Gypsy, the Egyptian High Priestess, the Monk. In discovering her true self she has tapped into that timeless presence--full of energy and wisdom--so often missed in our day-to-day lives.

In finding herself, she has also identified her true calling, which is to help others discover who they are, why they're here, and what they're going to do about it. It's the ultimate marriage of ability and opportunity. She has found her voice--honest, ageless, beautiful, mystical--and it's her passion to help others do the same.

Her professional life has fed this passion. For more than a decade she has guided clients and audiences to recognize their inner gifts and identify their true callings. A Reiki Master, she has worked with terminally ill patients and was the resident Reiki practitioner for a Seattle AIDS facility. In addition to Mystic Mommy, she has written numerous articles for regional and national publications. She is in demand both in private practice and for lectures and workshops because she can see the light within you, and guide you to your own gifts and callings.

Cat makes her home in Sedona, Arizona.